The New Evangelism
and Other Papers
by Henry Drummond

With the exception of the article on "The Contribution of Science to Christianity," which appeared in The Expositor, none of the following papers were intended for publication, nor were they revised by the Author. In a few cases portions of the manuscript are missing, and such omissions are shown by asterisks.

Table of Contents

The New Evangelism: and its Relation to Cardinal Doctrines

Paper read to Free Church Theological Society, Glasgow.

It is no small heroism in these times to deal with anything new. But this is a theological society; and I do not need to ask the protection of that name while I move for a little among lines of thought which may seem to verge on danger. One does not need to apologize for any inquiry made in a formative school of theology such as this; for in this atmosphere a seeker after truth is compelled to take up another than that provincial stand-point which elsewhere he is committed to.

The question you will naturally ask at the outset is, What is the new Evangelism? Now that is a question that I cannot answer. I do not know what the new Evangelism is, and it is because I do not know that I write this paper. I write because I ought to know, and am trying to know. Many here, and all the most earnest minds of our Church, are anxiously asking this question, and each who has once asked it feels it to be one of the chief objects of his life to answer it.

Preachers, finding that the things which stirred men's minds two centuries ago fail to do so now are compelled to ask themselves what this means. Do we need a new Evangelism, and if so, what? By the word Evangelism I do not mean to include merely, or even particularly, evangelistic work, evangelistic meetings, or what is comprehended under the general head of revivalism. I mean the methods of presenting Christian truth to men's minds in any form. By the new Evangelism, so far as mere definition is concerned, is meant the particular substance and form of evangel which is adapted to the present state of men's minds. The new Evangelism, in a word, is the Gospel for the Age. To notice the outcry against the mere mention of a Gospel for the Age is unnecessary here. What do we want with a new Gospel? Can the Gospel ever be old? might be asked elsewhere, for this is always cast in one's teeth when he raises those questions, as if by speaking of a new Evangelism he was depreciating the old Gospel. Of course we do not want a new evangel, we state that out at once; but an Evangelism is a different thing, and we do want that; we want that at the present hour, almost above any reform of our time.

I. The need of a new Evangelism.

There are two general considerations which seem to me to prove the need of a new Evangelism.

The first is the threatened decline of vital religion under present methods of preaching. If the Gospel be the power of God unto salvation, we are entitled to believe that wherever it is presented to men's minds it will influence and impress them. If men are not influenced or impressed under preaching, the only alternatives are, either that the Gospel in substance is not the power of God unto salvation, or that the Gospel in form is not presented to them so as to reach them. Either the Gospel cannot save them, or the Gospel does not reach them. We, as Christians, are shut up to the latter. The Gospel is not reaching men. There are hundreds of churches where the Gospel is not reaching men. Every third minister one meets confesses that. The Church, as a whole, admits, for instance, that she is rapidly losing hold of young men as a class. What does that mean? It really means that the Gospel, as presented to them, has ceased to be a gospel; it is neither good nor new. It means that the active thinkers of a congregation, the most hopeful and eager, are failing to find anything there to meet their case. It is not simply that many of them object to religion naturally, which will always be the case, but that those who are looking for a religion do not find it. Many of ourselves know this by our own experience. How long did we not search; on what diverse ministries did we not wait; to what endless volumes did we not turn; before finding a message which our faith could grasp or conscience rest on, and at the same time our intelligence respect? "I like Christianity," said Hallam, the subject of Tennyson's "In Memoriam," "because it fits into all the folds of one's nature." How long was it before we found a form of Christianity which fitted into any of the folds of our nature? From the time they were Sabbath-school scholars onwards, it is the experience of thousands of young men that they find only misfit after misfit in the theological clothes in which they were asked to disguise themselves. If this has been the experience of men who were not simply passive (men who were not simply waiting until religion would, some day or somehow, seize hold of them), but who were searching for religion, what substance is there in the present form of it to captivate the ordinary run of men? Our present Evangelism, as mere matter of fact, is not meeting the wants of the age.

In 1847 Dr. Chalmers found—and the statistics almost paralyzed him—that there were 30,000 people in Glasgow who did not go to church. Since then the Free Church has risen; Baptists, Independents, Morisonians, and Wesleyans, have poured their new life into the city. The most complete evangelistic organization in the kingdom, the Christian Union, has been at work. Have Chalmers' 30,000 been sensibly reduced? They have been increased exactly fivefold—out of-all proportion to the increase of the population. Excluding 100,000 Roman Catholics, there are at present 150,000 non-church-goers in the city. The aspect of affairs in the English towns is notoriously worse. To take a single case. The population of Sheffield is 240,000. It has 60 churches. Allowing 1,000 sitters to each church there would only be accommodation for 60,000 people; not only, therefore, do 180,000 not go to church, but there is no accommodation for them if they were willing. What is the cause of this

decline in vital religion? Why is the Gospel not reaching the Age? Because
it is not the Gospel for the Age. It is the Gospel for a former Age. Because,
in the form of it as used, the Gospel is neither good nor new. It does not
fit into all the folds of men's being. It is not in itself bad—but it is a bad
fit.

The second general consideration is based, not on the effects of
Evangelism, but on its nature. The very nature of truth demands from
time to time a new Evangelism. At the opening of this college, we heard
(Prof. Bruce's introductory lecture) that a Scotch divine at the
Presbyterian Council in Philadelphia found himself rebuked for using the
phrase, "Progress in Theology." Theology, he was eloquently reminded,
was behind us. He was pointed to the Standards of his Church. There is
no more unfortunate word in our Church's vocabulary than "Standard."
A standard is a thing that stands. Theology is a thing that moves. There
must be progress in everything, and more in theology than in anything,
for the content of theology is larger and more expansive than the content
of anything else. I do not say we are to give up the idea involved in the
word Standard. We certainly never can. But standards must move. The
sole condition of having them with us at any particular place or time is
that they should move with us according to place or time. The word
Standard, as applied to theology, is in some respects an unfortunate term.
Buffon's Natural History was a standard. Linnaeus' Vegetable System
was a standard. But they are not standards now. They were places for the
mind of Science to rest on in its onward sweep through the centuries; but
the perches are not needed there now, and they are vacant. These books
stand like deserted inns on the roadside which gave hearty meals and
shelter in their day, but which the race (with no disrespect to Linnaeus
and Buffon) has long since passed. When the English fought Waterloo,
they did not leave their standard at Bannockburn—they brought it up to
Quatre Bras; and if our standard was made for Holland, or Rome, or
Geneva, we must bring it up to Germany, and Paris, and the Highlands.
But there is something deeper than progress in theology; there is progress
in truth itself. "Truth is the daughter of Time." It is surely unnecessary
to insist on this, for it is true of all kinds of truth, in the natural as well
as the spiritual sphere. Nature is all before our eyes, as truth in the Bible
is all before our eyes. But we do not see it all; every day we are seeing
more. The firmament was not all mapped by astronomers at once. Since
Calvin's time many a new star has been discovered. The stars were there
before. Space was there before, but a new order is seen in it, new material
for thought, new systems, especially a new perspective. To take another
illustration: when we were children we could not understand how, if God
made the world, He had made it so ugly; why everything in nature was
brown, or dun, or green, and grey. Why was the sky not scarlet like the
inside of our trumpet, or a good hearty blue, with unicorns on it like our
drum? We thought, as we looked at the lichens and washed-out azure,
that, by some oversight, God had forgotten to put the colour in. We know
now why God did not put the colour in. We know that Nature wears the
colour of the future. It is painted for the highest art. Vermilion is for the

savage, blue with unicorns for the child, the neutral tints for the world's maturity—the developed taste. The colour was in Nature all along, but the world's eye was not full grown. The Greeks had almost no colour-sense at all; and if Mr. Ruskin sees what Homer did not see, it is not because it was not to be seen, but that the faculty was not developed.

The higher art has grown; it sees in the colouring of Nature a beauty which must increase till the evolution of mind and eye pronounces and sees all perfect. It is so with Truth; the truth-sense, like the colour-sense, grows. Truth has her vermilion, and her high art olives and sage-greens. "When Solon was asked," says Plutarch, "if he had given the Athenians the best possible laws, he answered that they were as good as the people could then receive." When we were given our system of truth, it was as good as the people could receive—perhaps as good as their teachers could give. But we can receive more now; our taste demands sage-green, and we cannot live on vermilion. If it be objected that this argument renders the Bible itself effete, the answer is that the Bible is not a system. It is the firmament; its truth is without form, therefore without limit. It is a book of such boundless elasticity that the furthest growth of the truth-sense can never find its response outgrown. And it is in this elasticity that one finds a sanction for a new theology to be the basis of a new Evangelism. It encourages a new theology; the prospect and possibility of that is written in every epigram and paradox, in the absence of anything propositional or bound. The view we are to take, therefore, of the old theologies is not that they are false, but simply that they are old. Those who framed them did in their time just what we want to do in ours. The Reformation did not profess to create new truth; it was not a re-formation, but simply a restoration—a restoration of the first theology of the New Testament, as much of it as could then be seen. At the time, probably, it was a restoration, and had all the strength and grandeur of the first theology, with all its vividness and life. Probably it was suited to the wants of the time, and moved the hearts of preacher and people.

We, too, can still preach it, but to some of us it has a hollow sound. If we would confess the honest truth, our words for it are rather those of respect than enthusiasm; we read it, hear it, study it, and preach it, but cannot honestly say that it kindles or moves us. When we wish to be kindled or moved, driven perhaps to prove whether we are capable of being kindled or moved, we leave the restoration and go back to that which was restored.

Restoration can only retain its hold vitally and powerfully for a limited time. It is essentially an accommodation for a certain age. If that age has changed, it no longer accommodates me, it incommodes me. What was the new theology of the seventeenth century is the theology of the nineteenth century only on one condition—that the age has not grown. If it has, in the nature of things it no longer accommodates me. It is not bad, simply a bad fit. The then new theology, the very adaptation possibly that was needed, becomes now old doctrine, a mere old skull, an old skull with the juices dry. This is the source of what is called dry preaching. It is a once glorious truth disenchanted by time into a faded, juiceless form.

Such then is the general effect of Time on Truth. As the serpent periodically casts its skin, so Truth. The number of times it has cast its skin marks the number of stages in its forward growth. Many of the shelves of our theological libraries are simply museums of the cast skin of Truth. The living organism has glided out of them to seek a roomier vestment. This is no disrespect, I repeat again, to the old theology. For the present vestiture in turn must take its place on the shelf. Nor does it imply that no beauty exists there, nor that to many some of the old doctrines may not prove even to-day a fountain of life. They do do so. Many volumes of theology have never been outgrown; many of the Puritans, for instance, have not only never been outgrown, but it is difficult to conceive how they can be. To take again the analogy from colour. The sage-green does not necessarily destroy the vermilion, though it renders many of its combinations old-fashioned. Some forms of truth in like manner may have reached their ultimate expression, certainly they may, though this is not so clear as that some have not. To sum up, the demand for a new theology, therefore, as the basis of a new Evangelism is founded upon the nature of Truth. It is not caprice, nor love of what is new. It is the necessity for what is new. It is in the nature of things.

I have next to bring some more specific charges against the old theology—the old theology, that is to say, as represented in the ordinary preaching of the day. And lest I should be accused of caricaturing the doctrines in question, let me say that the rendering which follows represents the impression made as matter of fact by these doctrines upon myself. I do not implicate the whole Evangelism, nor do I speak directly for any one else; but I cannot more honestly illustrate the teaching of what was to me the current Evangelism—the pabulum, namely, supplied by the ordinary country pulpit, by the evangelist's address, by the Sabbath-school teacher, and in a limited sense by religious books and tracts—than by stating the sort of religious ideas which these fostered in myself. For convenience I select three as samples, taking them in theological order. I limit myself likewise to a very few sentences with regard to each, more particularly (1) as to the theological conception and (2) as to the ethical effect.

(1) *the conception of God* as fostered by the old Evangelism.

The chief characteristic of the conception of God to me was its want of characteristic. The figure was too vague for any practical purpose. It was not a character. One could form no intelligent figure of God, for so far as it could be formed it was the God of the Old Testament. The Incarnation, i.e., contributed nothing. The Old Testament believer, I need not remind you, was very helpless as to a personal God. Each man, practically, had to make an image of God for himself. He was given a name, and a set of qualities—Holiness, Justice, Wisdom, and others, and out of this he had to make God. The consequence was that the great majority made it wrong, and worshipped they knew not what. One great purpose of the Incarnation was to change all this. It is to give us a new, defined, intelligible Figure of God. "The Son of God is come." said John, who saw most fully the meaning of the Word made Flesh—"The Son of God is come, and hath given us an understanding that we may know him."

The old Evangelism had little benefit here from the incarnation in this respect. It never got this understanding. God remained unchristianized in it. The Figure came no nearer. God remained Jehovah, the I AM that I *Am*. He was not God in Christ, God made intelligible by Christ, God made lovable by Christ, but God Eternal, Unchangeable, Invisible, therefore Unknowable; and in the nature of this cloud-God, the outstanding element was Vengeance —Anger, the ethical effect of which is obvious. A man's whole religion depends on his conception of God, so much so that to give a man religion in many cases is simply to correct his conception of God. But if man's natural conception of God, which is of a Being or of a Force opposed to him, a Being to be appeased, be not corrected, his religion will be a religion of Fear. God therefore was a God to be feared, an uncomfortable presence about one's life. He was always in court, either actually sitting in judgment or collecting material for the next case. He was the haunting presence of a great Recorder,

"Who was writing now the story
Of what little children do."

The reiteration that God was Love did nothing to dispel this terrible illusion. We cannot love God because we are told, for Love is not made to order. We can believe God's love, but believing love is like looking at heat. We cannot respond to it. To excite love, we need a person, not a doctrine—a Father, not a deity. To be changed into the same image we must look at the glory of God, not in se, but in the face of Jesus. The old Evangelism was defective in not exhibiting God in the face of Jesus. It exhibited God in the nailed hands of Jesus; this is an aspect of God, an essential aspect, but not God. Next—

(2) *the conception of Christ.*

If the conception of God was vague, the conception of Christ was worse. He was a theological person. His function was to adjust matters between the hostile kingdoms of heaven and earth.

I do not acquit myself of blame here, and I hope no one else has an experience so shocking, but until well on in my college course, and after hearing hundreds of sermons and addresses on the Person and Work of Christ, the ruling idea left in my mind was that Christ was a mere convenience. He was the second person in the Trinity, existing for the sake of some logical or theological necessity, a doctrinal convenience. He was the creation of theology, and His function was purely utilitarian. This might have been theological, but it was not religious. Religion said, "Christ our Life." Theology said, "Christ our Logic."

This is a painful confession, but it is far more painful to think of its basis. It is impossible to believe that in these sermons I was not presented with the true aspects of Christ's life and character. But it is also almost impossible to believe that these were insisted on with anything like the same frequency or reality as the aspect I have named. What moves an attentive mind in a sermon is its residual truth, not the complementary passages, not the squarings with other doctrines, but that truth on which the whole theme is strung, the vertebral column which, though hid, is the true pillar of the rest. Now the residuum to me—and it is surprising how unerringly this betrays itself and stands nakedly out from all mere words—was always this. Whatever other points were thrown in, whatever devout expressions were mixed with it, whatever appeals to the affections, this was the prominent half-truth, and therefore whole error.

This is the explanation, I think, of the fact, now pretty well acknowledged, that the old theology made almost nothing of the humanity of Christ. In such a body of divinity clearly there was little room for so mundane a thing as humanity. The arrangements in which Christ played a part were looked at almost exclusively from the Divine and cosmical standpoint. The question was, how God could forgive sin, and yet justify the sinner; how God could do this and that, as if we had anything to do with it. Such a divinity necessarily wanted humanity, the humanity of man as well as the humanity of Christ. Man was a cypher, the mere theological unit, the x of doctrine (his character, his aims, his achievements, his influence, were neither here nor there) and an unknown quantity, one of the parties in the proposition. And it was not necessary for this theological unit to have a humanitarian Christ, except as to the mere identity of flesh, and this was requisite only to complete the theological proposition.

The emphasis on the humanity of Christ, which, happily, has now crept into our best teaching, marks more distinctly perhaps than anything else the dawn of the new Evangelism. Still, it must be confessed that in influential quarters the revival of this doctrine is viewed even yet with no inconsiderable alarm The newer Lives of Christ, for instance, in which the humanity is conspicuously developed, are constantly assailed as Unitarian, and within the last fortnight a Life of Christ has been given to the world, from the preface to which one can almost gather that the author's object is to provide an antidote to the erroneous tendencies of these works.

Men fail to see that it was God Himself who conceived this wonderful idea of a humanitarian Christ. When God does anything, He never does it by halves. When He made the Word flesh, when He made Jesus a Man, He made a Man, and it is just because He carried out His idea so perfectly that Unitarianism is possible. When we say Man, then let us mean Man. It is a mistaken scruple even to minimize His Humanity. In our zeal for the doctrines of the Atonement we are really robbing God of His doctrine of the Incarnation.

(3) A third point to notice is, The old Evangelism in its *conception of salvation*, and of religion generally. The characteristic to notice here is that religion was not so much a question of character as of status. Man's standing in the sight of God was the great thing. Was he sheltered judicially behind Christ, or was he standing on his own merits? This is a vital question to ask, certainly, but the way in which legal status was put sanctioned the most erroneous notions as to religion and life. Salvation was a thing that came into force at death. It was not a thing for life. Good

works, of course, were permitted, and even demanded, but they were never very clearly reconcilable with grace. The prime end of religion was to get off; the plan of salvation was an elaborate scheme for getting off; and after a man had faced that scheme, understood it, acquiesced in it, the one thing needful was secured. Life after that was simply a waiting until the plan should be executed by his death. What use life was, this one thing being adjusted, it were hard to say. It was not in the religious sphere at all. The world was to pass away, and the lust thereof, and all time given to it, all effort spent on it, was so much loss, like putting embroidery upon a shroud.

When a preacher did speak of character, of the imitation of Christ, of self-denial, of righteousness, of truth and humility, the references theologically were not only not clear, but were generally introduced with an apology for enforcing them at all. Nine times out of ten, too, the preacher took them all back under the last head, where he spoke of man's inability and the necessity of the Holy Spirit. The ethical effect of even weakening the absolute connection between religion and morality is too obvious to be referred to, so I shall pass on.

Having now given samples of the teaching of the old Evangelism, I need not take up the time to complete its circle of theology, for the doctrines indicated rule and colour all the rest. No doubt what has been said up till now is more or less commonplace to most of you, and (with regard to the more) I now proceed to attempt something more constructive, for which, however, all that has gone before has been a somewhat necessary preparation. In what follows I can only hope to indicate what dimly seem to me to be the lines upon which a new, intelligent, and living Evangelism must be built up.

II. What I am most anxious to do here is to arrive at principles. I make no attempt to sketch portions of a detailed theology, such as one might wish to see taking the place of some of the old doctrines. That will all come in time; i.e., if it ought to come. It is the principles which are to guide us in constructing the new Evangelism that are the true difficulty. We have all our own opinion as to special points of contrast, and, as we think, of improvement; but what outstanding general truths are to regulate the movement as a whole? I fear I shall only have time to refer to two.

(1) Perhaps the most important principle, in the first place, is that the new Evangelism must not be doctrinal. By this is not meant that it is to be independent of doctrine, but simply that its truths as conveyed to the people are not to be in the propositional form. With regard to doctrine, to avoid misconception, let me say at once we must recognise it as one of the three absolutely essential possessions of a Christian Church.

The three outstanding departments of the Church's work are criticism, dogmatism, and Evangelism. Without the first there is no guarantee of truth, without the second there is no defence of truth, and without the third there is no propagation of truth. Criticism then, in a word, secures truth, dogmatism conserves it, and evangelism spreads it. Now, when it is said that preaching is not to be doctrinal, what is meant is this. When Evangelism wishes to receive truth, so as to expound it, it is to refer to criticism for information rather than to dogmatism. And when it gives out what it has received, it is neither to be critical in form, nor doctrinal.

To deal with this in detail. When Evangelism wishes to receive truth in order to expound it, it is to refer to criticism for that truth rather than to dogmatism. This simply means that a man is to go to a reliable edition of the Bible for his truth, and not to theology.

Why should he take this trouble? Does not theology give him Bible truth in accurate, convenient, and, moreover, in logical propositions? There it lies ready made to his hand, all cut and dry; why should he not use it? Just because it is all cut and dry. Just because it lies there ready made in accurate, convenient, and logical propositions. You cannot cut and dry truth. You cannot accept truth ready made without its ceasing to live as truth. And that is one of the reasons why the current Evangelism is dead.

There is in reality no worse enemy under certain circumstances to a true Evangelism than a propositional theology, with the latter controlling the former by the authority of the Church. For one does not then receive the truth for himself; he accepts it bodily. He begins, set up by his Church with a stock in trade which has cost him nothing, and which, though it may serve him all his life, is just as much worth exactly as his belief in his Church. One effect of this is to relieve him of all personal responsibility. This possession of truth, moreover, thus lightly won, is given to him as infallible. There is nothing to add to it. It is a system. And to start a man in life with such a principle is a degradation. All through life, instead of working towards truth, he is working from it, or what he is told is it.

An infallible standard is a temptation to a mechanical faith. Infallibility always paralyzes. It gives rest, but it is the rest of stagnation. Men make one great act of faith at the beginning of their lives—then have done with it for ever. All moral, intellectual, and spiritual effort is over; and a cheap theology ends in a cheap life. It is the same thing that makes men take refuge in the Church of Rome and in a set of dogmas. Infallibility meets the deepest desire of man, but meets it in the most fatal form. All desire is given to stimulate to action; much more this, the deepest,—the hunger after truth. Men deal with this desire in two ways. First, by Unbelief,—that crushes it by blind force; second, by Infallibility,—that lulls it to sleep by blind faith. The effect of a doctrinal theology is the effect of infallibility. The wholesale belief in a system, however grand it may be, grant even that it were infallible—the wholesale belief in this system as the starting point for a working Evangelism is not Faith, though it always gets that name. It is mere credulity. There is a vital difference between Faith and credulity. Realize what it fully amounts to, and you will see how much, besides this, there is in the religion of this country which falls before the distinction. There is no real religious value in this belief; for it is more belief in a Church than in truth. It is a comfortable, credulous rest upon authority, not a hard-earned, self-obtained personal possession Truth never becomes truth until it is earned. The moral responsibility here, besides, is nothing. The Westminster Divines are responsible, not I. And anything which destroys responsibility, or transfers it, cannot but be injurious in its moral tendency, and useless in itself.

It may be objected, perhaps, that this statement of the paralysis, spiritual and mental, induced by infallibility applies also to the Bible. The answer is that though the Bible is infallible, the infallibility is not in such a form as to become a temptation. And that leads to a remark as to the contrast between the form of truth in the Bible and the form in theology. In theology, as we have seen, truth is propositional, tied up in neat parcels, systematized and arranged in logical order. In the Bible, truth is a fountain. There is an atmosphere here, an expansiveness, an infinity. Theology is essentially finite, and it only contains as much infinite truth as can be chained down by its finite words. The very point of it is, that it is defined, otherwise it is no use.

To the practical question. There are few minds which can really take truth in this theological form. Truth is a thing to be slowly absorbed, not to be bolted whole. In this country we have been so accustomed to get and give our truth in the propositional form, that many congregations do not recognise it if stated in the ordinary language of life. But this is the only living language. And the failure to catch sight of the truth when clothed in this language means that it has not been comprehended before as a substance, but as a form.

"Two or three days ago, I dined," says Lynch in "Letters to the Scattered," "with a little child whose mamma had prepared for him a very wholesome and delightful pudding. `what is in it?' said the child. `There's an egg in it,' said the mother. `Where's the egg?' asked the child, after close and incredulous inspection. `It is mixed with it,' she explained."

"There are many grown men and women," adds Lynch, "that unless they see the very form of a doctrine will not believe they can have the nutriment of it. They ask, `Where's the egg?' and if you say it is mixed with it—the doctrine of Atonement, or of Justification, or Sanctification—and was diffused through the whole of what was said, they shake their heads suspiciously. They will have nothing to do with such preaching, or such books, or such people."

There is nothing truer, certainly, than that in this country people at once suspect adulteration if you do not present them with the actual egg, shell and all. But what I am trying to show is that this demand is a mistake, and defeats its own end. The truth is Nature never provides for man's wants in any direction, bodily, mental, or spiritual, in such a form as that he can simply accept her gifts automatically. She puts all the mechanical powers at his disposal, but he must make his lever. She gives him corn, but he must grind it. She prepares coal, but he must dig it; and even when she grows him apples and plums, ready-made fruits, he has at least to digest them, and in most cases he had better cook them. A law of nature like this, we are justified in carrying by analogy into the region of the spiritual. A man can no more assimilate truth in infallible lumps than he can corn. Though it be perfect, infallible, yet he has to do everything to it before he can use it. Corn is perfect, all the products of Nature are perfect, and perfection in Nature corresponds to infallibility in truth. But perfect though they are, few of the products of Nature are available as they stand. So with Truth. Man must separate, think, prepare, dissolve, digest, work, and most of these he must do for himself and within himself. If it be replied that this is exactly what theology does, I answer, it is exactly what it does not. It simply does what the greengrocer does when he arranges his apples and plums in the shop-windows. He may tell me a Magnum Bonum from a Victoria, or a Baldwin from a Newtown Pippin; but he does not help me to eat it. His information is useful, and for scientific horticulture absolutely essential. Should a sceptical pomologist deny that there was such a thing as a Baldwin or mistake it for a Newtown Pippin, we should be glad to refer the said pomologist to him. But if we were hungry, and an orchard were handy, we should not trouble him. This brings us back to the original proposition then, that the new Evangelism as a provision for the hunger of men's souls is not to be doctrinal. Their truth is to be given them, not in infallible lumps, but as a diffused nutriment. Truth is an orchard rather than a museum. Dogmatism will be very useful to us when scientific necessity makes us go to the museum. Criticism will be very useful in seeing that only fruit-bearers grow in the orchard and neither weeds nor poisonous sports. But truth in infallible propositional lumps is not natural, proper, assimilable food for the soul of man; and therefore a propositional theology is not the subject-matter of Evangelism.

(2) So much for exposition of the nature of the truth with which Evangelism is concerned. The second principle to which we now turn refers to a matter of equal moment—the faculty which deals with truth. And I might sum up what is to be said under this head in this proposition—The leading Faculty of the new theology is not to be the Reason. The previous proposition deals with the form of truth. This is meant to elucidate the principle of arriving at truth. It is a deeper question, and strikes at a fundamental difference between the old and the new theology.

The old theology was largely a product of reason. It was an elaborate, logical construction. The complaint against it is that, as a logical construction, it was arrived at by a faculty of the mind, and not by a faculty of the soul. On close scrutiny it turns out to be really nothing more nor less than rationalism.

The doctrine of the Atonement, for instance, and the whole federal theology is an elaborate rationalism. The common way of presenting salvation is the most naked syllogism: "I believe. He that believeth hath everlasting life, therefore I have everlasting life." I do not pause to point out that a theology of this sort may be received by any one without any spiritual effect whatsoever being produced. It does not take a religious man to be a theologian; it simply takes a man with fair reasoning powers. This man happens to apply these powers to doctrinal subjects, but in no other sense than he might apply them to astronomy or physics. I knew a man, the author of a well-known orthodox theological work which has passed through a dozen editions, and lies on the shelves of all our libraries. I never knew that man to go to church, nor to give a farthing in charity, though he was a rich man, nor to give any sensible sign whatever that he had ever heard of Christianity. It is equally unnecessary to point out that if reason is the exclusive or primary faculty in theology, theology itself breaks down under rigid tests at almost every point. Its first principle, for example, that God is, contains a distinct contradiction, as has been repeatedly pointed out. Many philosophers, therefore, in being presented with theology as the expression of the Christian religion, have had no alternative but to become atheists. The reasoning faculty then cannot be the organ of the new Evangelism, for its conclusions are philosophically assailable. But I am not dealing here with philosophy, and it is not to be understood that I am using terms—Reason, for instance—in any particular philosophical sense. I am looking at the question exclusively from its practical side. And the question I ask myself is, "When I apprehend spiritual truth, what faculty do I employ?" When I say it is not the reason, I do not purposely make the distinction between the Understanding and the Reason, which Kant and his followers, for example, do in philosophy, and Coleridge in religion, making the Understanding the logical faculty and the Reason the intuitive faculty. I use the word in its ordinary working sense, meaning by it, if you like, the logical understanding of the writer's mind.

What faculty do I employ, then, in apprehending spiritual truth? What is the primary faculty of the new Evangelism if it is not the Reason? Leaving philosophical distinctions aside again, I think it is the IMAGINATION. Overlook the awkwardness of this mere word, and ask yourself if this is not the organ of your mind which gives you a vision of truth. The subject-matter of the new Evangelism must be largely the words of Christ, the circle of ideas of Christ in their harmony, and especially in their perspective. Sit down for a moment and hear Him speak. Take almost any of His words. To what faculty do they appeal? Almost without exception to the Imagination. And this is the main thing I wish to say to-night. I do not merely refer to His parables, to His allusions to nature, to the miracles, to His endless symbolism—the comparisons between Himself and bread, water, vine, wine, shepherd, doctor, light, life, and a score of others. But all His most important sayings are put up in such form as to make it perfectly clear that they were deliberately designed for the Imagination.

You cannot indeed really put up religious truth in any other form. You can put up facts, information, but God's truth will not go into a word. You must put it in an image. God Himself could not put truth in a word, therefore He made the Word flesh. There are few things less comprehended than this relation of truth to language.

"Was stets und aller Orten
Sich ewig jung erweist
Ist in gebundnen Worten
Ein ungebundner Geist."

The purpose of revelation is to exhibit the mind of God—the ungebundner Geist. The vehicle is words, gebundnen Worten. What words? Words which are windows and not prisons. Words of the intellect cannot hold God—the finite cannot hold the infinite. But an image can. So God has made it possible for us by giving us an external world to make image-words. The external world is not a place to work in, or to feed in, but to see in. It is a world of images, the external everywhere revealing the eternal. The key to the external world is to look not at the things which are seen but in looking at the things which are seen to see through them to the things that are unseen. Look at the ocean. It is mere water—a thing which is seen; but look again, look through that which is seen, and you see the limitlessness of Eternity. Look at a river, another of God's images of the unseen. It is also water, but God has given it another form to image a different truth. There is Time, swift and silent. There is Life, irrevocable, passing. But the most singular truth of this, as suggested a moment ago, is the Incarnation. There was no word in the world's vocabulary for Himself. In Nature we had images of Time and Eternity. The seasons spoke of Change, the mountains of Stability. The home-life imaged Love. Law and Justice were in the civil system. The snow was Purity, the rain, Fertility. By using these metaphors we could realize feebly Time and Eternity, Stability and Change. But there was no image of Himself. So God made one. He gave a word in Flesh—a word in the Image-form. He gave the Man Christ Jesus the express image of His person This was the one image that was wanting in the image-vocabulary of truth, and the Incarnation supplied it.

God had really supplied this image before, but man had spoilt it, disfigured it to such an extent that it was unrecognisable. God made man in His own image; that was a word made flesh. From its ruins man might have reconstructed an image of God, but the audacity of the attempt repelled him, and for centuries men had forgotten that the image of God was in themselves.

How, then, do you characterize that irreverent elaboration of theology which attempts to show you in words what God has had to do in the slow unfolding of Himself in history, and by that final resort, when words were useless, of incarnating the Word, giving us the manifestation of a living God in a living Word. These doctrines stand apart. They are above words. It is a mockery for the Reason to define and formulate here, as if by heaping up words she could drive the truth into a corner and dispense it in phrases as required. It is just as clear as a simple question of rhetoric, that Christ's words were positively protected against the mere touch of reason. They were put up in such form in many cases as to challenge reason to make beginning, middle, or end of them. Try to reason out a parable. Try to read into it theology, as our forefathers often did; or dispensational truth, as certain erratic theologians do to-day, and it becomes either utterly contemptible or utterly unintelligible.

You see a parable, you discern it; it enters your mind as an image, you image it, imagine it. I am the Bread of Life. With what faculty do we apprehend that? We look at it long and earnestly, and at first are utterly baffled by it. But as we look it grows more and more transparent, and we see through it. We do not understand it; if we were asked what we saw, we should be surprised at the difficulty we had in defining it. Some image rose out of the word Bread, became slowly living, sank into our soul, and vanished. The peculiarity of this expression is that it is not a simile. "I am like bread." Christ does not say that. I am bread—the thing itself. And that faculty, standing face to face with truth, draws aside the veil, or pierces it, seizes the living substance, absorbs it; and the soul is nourished.

Besides the parable, the metaphor, and the metaphor which is no metaphor, Christ has two other favourite modes of expression. These are the axiom and the paradox. The axiom is the basis of certainty; the reason is inoperative without it, but it is not apprehended by reason. It is seen, not proved. Again, therefore, we are dealing with the Imagination. The paradox is the darkest of all figures. "He that loveth his life shall lose it, and he that hateth his life shall find it." What can reason make of that? It is an utter blank; it absolutely repels reason. But for that very cause it is the richest mine for the imagination. It is not the darkest figure, but the lightest, because the rays come from exactly opposite sides, and meet as truth in the middle. The shell of words, once burst, reveals a whole world, in which the illuminated mind runs riot, and revels in the boundlessness of truth.

Had the reason been able to sink its shaft, it might have brought up a nugget. Theology would have gained another proposition, another neat parcel, and there would have been the end of it. As it is, it is without end, limitless, infinite truth, incapable in that form of becoming uninteresting, unreal, included in a human phrase. It is this sense of depth about Christ's words which is the sure test of their truth. They shade off, every one, into the unknown, and the roots of the known are always in the unknown. Omnia exeunt in mysterium. Dogma is simply an attempt to undo this. It takes up the sublimest truth in its fingers with no more awe than an anatomist lifts a muscle with his forceps, turns it about, dissects it, determines the genus and species of the organism to which it belongs, and marks it down "described" for all future time. We know all about it—all about it. We see the whole thing quite clearly; it is as simple as the frog's muscle. The new Evangelism can never deal with truth in this way. It will never say that it sees quite clearly. It may remain ignorant, but it will never presume to say there is no darkness, no mystery, no unknown. It will sound truth, it will go fathoms further perhaps than the reason can go, but it will come back saying we have found no bottom. It is not all as clear as the old theology; it has that dimness of an older theology which sees through a glass darkly, which knows in part, and which, because it knows in part, knows the more certainly that it shall know hereafter.

The want of apprehension of the quality of truth by much of the propositional theology is in nothing better evidenced than by this mistake as to its quantity. It robbed it at once of the infinite and the supernatural. The soul-food was taken out of the truth, and the husks thrown to the intellect. As a faculty, then, the reason is not large enough to be the organ of Christianity. It has a very high and prominent place to play in Christianity, but prima facie it lacks the first and the second qualities of a religious faculty. The first of these qualities is that just mentioned, largeness and penetration. The second is universality. All men cannot reason, but all men can see. In the rudest savage and in the youngest child, the imagination is strong. And Christ addressed His religion to the most unlettered, to the youngest child. He boldly asserted that His religion was for the youngest child. He directly appealed again and again to the child-spirit. "Except ye become as a little child, ye shall in no wise enter into the kingdom of heaven." To object to this that Christ was speaking to the Oriental mind is of course beside the mark. Christ was not an Oriental speaking to the Oriental, He was the Son of Man speaking to man in the universal language of truth. I have already apologised for using this word Imagination, but I think I have made clear the idea. I am not concerned longer, therefore, about retaining it. I am not sure that it is the right word. You might perhaps prefer to call it faith or intuition, or the spirit of discernment, or a subjective idealism, but the name is of no moment. The idea I have tried to make clear is that this is the faculty which works with the eyes, as contrasted with reason, which works with the hands. The old theology manipulates truth, the new is to discern it. As preachers our aim must be, not to prove things, but to make men see things.

This conclusion with regard to the faculty of the new Evangelism is derived simply from observation. It contains the crucial point of the whole question, and I have little more to say except in support of it. But I need scarcely remind those of you who are in any way conversant with German philosophy that distinctions closely corresponding to this have been drawn in philosophy, and long indeed before the German philosophers arose. The later form of this philosophy filtered into English literature early in this century, and at once awakened profound interest, and, it is fair to say, alarm. Through such men as Coleridge and the Hares it was easily traced to its source in Schelling and Kant. But that Schelling and Kant, Fichte and Hegel had differentiated this faculty, or something like this faculty, in the philosophical sphere, was against it. The new influence for the time was quenched. The unfortunate thing with the English neo-Platonists was that they paid too little attention to the practical aspects of truth. Had Coleridge done this, had Maurice and Hare done this more, we should have been farther on to-day with the new Evangelism. These men, and especially Coleridge, were far too transcendental in their metaphysics to be the prophets of the new Evangelism, but with many other errors they held the germ of a very great truth. With Coleridge the imagination was a synthesis of the reasoning power and the sensing power. His definition is "that reconciling and mediatory power, which, incorporating the reason in images of sense, and organizing (as it were) the flux of the senses, by the permanent and self-circling energies of the reason, gives birth to a system of symbols harmonious in themselves, and consubstantial with the truths of which they are the conductors." Again he says "the grounds of the real truth, the life, the substance, the hope, the love, in one word the faith, these are derivatives from the practical, moral, and spiritual nature and being of man."

I do not stop to inquire here as to where Coleridge's version of "the Light which lighteth every man that cometh into the world" leads. The new Evangelism doubtless will have its apologetics when it exists. Nor do I enter upon the question as to how far this light exists in every man, or how far it is true that those only who are born again can see the kingdom of God. These are particular applications which may just now be passed over. But I should like to go on with the general subject by adding another quotation, this time from science, bearing upon the general subject.

In 1870 Professor Tyndall wrote an address entitled, "On the Scientific Use of the Imagination." The motto or text of this address is taken from a paper read before the Royal Society some years ago by its then president, Sir Benjamin Brodie. It says: "Physical investigation, more than anything besides, helps to teach us the actual value and right use of the imagination—that wondrous faculty which properly controlled by experience and reflection becomes the noblest attribute of man; the source of poetic genius, the instrument of discovery to science, without the aid of which Newton would never have invented fluxions, nor Davy have decomposed the earths and alkalies, nor would Columbus have found another continent." Then Tyndall goes on to say: "We find ourselves gifted with the power of forming mental images of the ultra-sensible; and by this power, when duly chastened and controlled, we can lighten the darkness which surrounds the world of the senses. There are Tories even in Science who regard Imagination as a faculty to be feared and avoided rather than employed." But "Imagination becomes the prime mover of the physical discoverer. Newton's passage from a falling apple to a falling moon was at the outset a leap of the Imagination. In Faraday the exercise of this faculty preceded all his experiments . . . . In fact, without this power our knowledge of Nature would be a mere tabulation of co-existences and sequences." If Tyndall claims so much for the scientific use of the Imagination, what may we not claim for the religious use of it? What is not possible to an Imagination guided by reason and illuminated, as we hold it may be, and is, by the Spirit of God? "Without this power," we might almost paraphrase from Tyndall, "our knowledge of religion must be, or is, a mere tabulation of co-existences and sequences." There is one preacher to whom, from his printed sermons, I have many times been much beholden and from whom I also quote a sentence. I do not stay to characterize the sermons of Horace Bushnell, but he has long been to me a representative man of the new Evangelism, although I knew nothing of him, of his life, of his methods of thought or work. But the other day he died, and his life was written. There I have found, to my great amazement, that Bushnell's method of looking at truth is defined by himself as an exercise of the Imagination. He has actually published an article, which appears in America bearing this title, "The Gospel a Gift to the Imagination." Permit me to quote a sentence or two from the biography. Bushnell is speaking in propria persona. "The Christian Gospel is pictorial. Its every line or lineament is traced in some image or metaphor, and no ingenuity can get it away from metaphor. No animal ever understood a metaphor. That belongs to man. . . . All the truths of religion are given by images, all God's revelation is made to the imagination, and all the rites, and services, and ceremonies of the olden times were only a preparation of draperies and figures for what was to come, the basis of words sometime to be used as metaphors of the Christian grace. 'Christ is God's last metaphor!' the express image of God's person! and when we have gotten all the metaphoric meanings of His life and death, all that is expressed and bodied in His person of God's saving help, and new-creating, sin-forgiving, reconciling love, the sooner we dismiss all speculations on the literalities of His incarnate miracles, His derivation, the composition of His person, His suffering, plainly transcendent as regards our possible understanding —the wiser we shall be in our discipleship. . . . If we try to make a science out of the altar metaphors, it will be no gospel that we make, but a poor dry jargon—(rather) a righteousness that makes nobody righteous, a justice satisfied by injustice, a mercy on the basis of pay, a penal deliverance that keeps on foot all the penal liabilities." One passage more. "There is no book in the world that contains so many repugnances or antagonistic forms of assertion as the Bible. Therefore, if any man please to play off his constructive logic upon it, he can easily show it up as the absurdest book in the world. But whosoever wants, on the other hand, really to behold, and receive all truth, and would have the truth-world overhang him as an empyrean of stars, complex, multitudinous, striving antagonistically, yet comprehended, height above height, and deep under deep in a boundless score of harmony—what man soever content with no small rote of logic and catechism, reaches with true hunger after this, and will offer himself to the many-sided forms of the Scripture with a perfectly ingenuous and receptive spirit, he shall find his nature flooded with senses, vastnesses and powers of truth such as it is even greatness to feel."

Gentlemen, after the old Evangelism, this is a new world to live in. There is air here. Take the Gospel as a gift to the Imagination, and you are entered into a large place. It is like a conversion. We read the Bible before with a key. A lamp was put in our hands with which to search for truth— rather to search for Scripture proofs of a truth thrust down our throats. We were not told the Bible was the lamp. I once saw an hotel-keeper on a starlit night in autumn erect an electric light to show his guests Niagara. It never occurred to the creature that God's dim, mystic starlight was ten million times more brilliant to man's soul than ten million carbons. When will it occur to us that God's truth is Light—self-luminous; to be seen because self-luminous? When shall we understand that it has no speech nor language, that men are to come to the naked truth with their naked eyes, bringing no candle? The old theology was luminous once. But it is not now. "Election," says Froude in "Bunyan," "Election, conversion, day of grace, coming to Christ, have been pawed and fingered by unctuous hands for near two hundred years. The bloom is gone from the flower. The plumage, once shining with hues direct from Heaven, is soiled and bedraggled. The most solemn of all realities have been degraded into the passwords of technical theology." It is from this that we are to emancipate ourselves, and, God helping us, others. We have a Gospel in the new Evangelism which for a hundred years the world has been waiting for. We have a Gospel which those who even faintly see it thank God that they live, and live to preach it. But I am not quite done yet. What will be, what are, the main hindrances to the acceptance of the new Evangelism? They are mainly two.

(1) Unspirituality and (2) Laziness.

(1) All formal religions are efforts to escape spirituality. It matters not what the form is—ritual, idols or doctrine, the essence of all is the same—they are devices to escape spiritual worship. The carnal mind is enmity against God—hates any spiritual exercise or effort. This is at the bottom of the perpetuation of the old theology. There is nothing a man will not do to evade spirituality. Do we not all know moods in which we would rather walk twenty miles than take family worship? And there are moods in which men find it of all efforts least easy to come into contact with living truth. This is always difficult: to know His doctrine, a man must do the will of God. The supreme factor in arriving at spiritual knowledge is not theology, it is consecration. But for years and years—and it is one of the saddest truths in this world—a preacher may go on manipulating his theological forms without the slightest exercise of religion, unknown to himself, and unnoticed by his people.

(2) The second obstacle is laziness. To make doctrinal sermons requires no effort. A man has simply to take down his Hodge, and there it is. Every Sabbath, though not formally expressed, he has the same heads. And the people understand it, or at least they understood it twenty years ago when he preached, and preached well and with real heart, in the bloom of his early ministry. But for years now he has been a mere mechanic, a repeater of phrases, a reproducer of Hodge. And the people—they too are spared all effort. They are delighted with their minister. He in these days preaches the Gospel.

A caution may be necessary. In His exhaustless wisdom, in speaking on these subjects the Lord Jesus said: "No man having tasted the old wine straightway desireth new." We can speak of these things broadly to one another here, but we cannot with too much delicacy insinuate the new Evangelism upon the Church. The old is better, men say; and if any man really feels that it is better, I do not know that we should urge it upon him at all. There are many saints in our Churches, and if the old wine is really their life-blood, we can but wish them Godspeed with all humility. Younger men will come to us, too, when our wine is old and the sun has set upon our new theology; but to the many who are waiting for the dawn, and these are many, our evangel may perhaps bring some light and fulfil gladness and liberty.

Least of all have we anything to do with wilfully destroying the old. Christ was never destructive in His methods. It was very exquisite tact, a true understanding of men and a delicate respect for them, that made Him say, "I came not to destroy but to fulfil."

The Method of the New Theology, and Some of its Applications

Address delivered to Theological Society of F. C. College, Glasgow, Jan., 1892.

I shall begin by congratulating you, and myself, on the free theological atmosphere in which it is the lot of this society to do its work. Never has there been fresher air in that dusty realm than there is to-day; and if we pay the price for our freedom in bewilderment or doubt, in the suspicion of our enemies, in the helplessness of our wisest friends to give us certainty, we have at least the sympathy of the best around us, and the stimulus of working in an age when theology is no longer stagnant, but the most living of all the sciences. Of what we seem to be leaving behind us we can speak without panic or regret. Much of what has been in faith or practice is visibly passing away. But there is little trace in this process of deliberate destruction; it resembles rather a natural decay. And it is the beauty of this change, and the guarantee of its wholesomeness, that it has worked without serious violence, that it has come, as all great kingdoms do, almost without observation.

Though this may appear to us a crisis, it is well to remind ourselves that to true thought crisis is chronic. There is nothing superior about ourselves that we shall have the privilege of thinking in a new way about theology. It is the world that progresses. Modern thought is not a new thing in history, nor is it an unrelated thing. It is simply the growing fringe of the coral reef, the bit of land far out, in contact on the one hand with the unexplored sea—the bit of land far out in the ocean of unexplored truth—on the other with the territory just taken in, and the place, in short, where busy minds are making the additions to what other busy minds have built through the ages into the growing continent of knowledge. After all, it is only the old reef that we extend; it is on the past we build; and the man who ignores the continuity of the past, and attempts to raise an island of his own, may be sure that the world's lease of it will be very short. New ideas are, in the main, a new light on old ideas, and nothing is gained by a ruthless handling of the older gospel which our fathers held and taught, and which for the most part made them better men than their sons.

But what is this newer theology, and what is the direction of the movement where changes and perturbations come home to us in such a society as this with so great an interest?

To some the new theology is a re-arrangement of doctrines in a new order, a bringing of those into prominence which suit the need and temper of the age, and an allowing of others to sink into shadow because they are either distasteful to this generation or rest on a basis which it will not honour. We are told, for example, that the accent in the modern gospel is placed no longer upon faith, but rather upon love. We are told by others that what they see is the intricate theology of Paul beginning to give place to the simpler theology of John, or both being for the time forgotten in the still simpler Christianity of Christ. To others the change is from the great Latin conception of the Divine Sovereignty of Augustine and Calvin to the earlier Greek theology, with its emphasis on the immanence of Christ, or to its renaissance in the nineteenth century presentation of the incarnation, and the Fatherhood of God.

But, important as these characterizations are, to contrast the subject-matter of the new and the old Evangelism is not enough. In a theological society we must get down to principles, and I wish in a word to state what seems to me the essential nature of this change, and to illustrate its practical value by plain examples.

The real contrast between the new and the old theology is one of method. The way to make a sermon on the old lines, for example, was to take down Hodge, or by an earlier generation Owen, and see what the truth was, then to work from that—to proclaim what Hodge said, to expound, assert, reiterate, appeal in the name of Hodge and anathematise and excommunicate everybody who did not agree with Hodge. The new method declines to begin with Hodge, or Owen, or even Calvin. It does not work from truth, but towards truth. It aims not at asserting a dogma, but at unearthing a principle. With all respect to authors, it yet declines authority. These are two at least of its more obvious marks— it does not only allow, but insists on the right of private judgment, and it declines authority. These propositions mean practically the same thing, and so far from being novelties are of the first essence of Protestantism.

It is only to re-assert these propositions in a different form to say that another characteristic of the new theology is its essential spirituality. We are accustomed to hear it opposed on spiritual grounds, but its spirituality is really its most outstanding feature, and as contrasted with some at least of the old theology it has the exclusive right to the name. The mark of the old theology was that it was made up of forms and propositions. Filled no doubt with spirit once, that spirit had in many instances wholly evaporated, and left men nothing to rest their souls on but a set of phrases.

The task of the newer theology has been to pierce below these phrases and seek out the ethical truth which underlay them: and having found that, to set up the words and phrases round it once more if possible; and where not possible, to set up new phrases and a more modern expression. It is of course because men have been accustomed to these old forms that they fail to recognise the truth when clothed in other expression, and therefore raise the cry of heresy against all who take the more inward or spiritual view.

Two classes in the community must of necessity, and always, oppose the new foundation—the Pharisee who is not able to see spirit for forms, and the lazy man who will not take the trouble to see spirit in form. It is always easier to assert truth than to examine it, to accept it ready made than to verify it for oneself, and we must always have a class who are guilty of these intellectual sins, who mistake credulity for faith and superstition for knowledge. The calm way in which these men assume that they are right and put all the rest of us on our defence is a miracle of effrontery, a miracle only exceeded in wonder by the tolerant way it is submitted to. I am not sure but that if Christ were among us He would not denounce the Pharisee as He did of old.

But it is not enough to say that the new theological quest is a movement in the direction of spirituality. What is that spirituality? Is it a mere vagueness, a substitution of the shifting sand of the mysterious, and the undefined for the buttressed logic of the older doctrines? On the contrary, it is the most definite thing in the world. Instead of relaxing the hold on truth, the new method makes the grasp of the mind upon it a thousand times more certain. Instead of blurring the vision of unseen things, it renders them self-transparent; instead of making acceptance a matter of mere opinion, or of upbringing, or of tradition, it forces truth on the mind with a new authority—an authority never before to the same extent introduced into theological teaching. That authority is the authority of law. The basis—like the basis of all modern knowledge—of the coming theology is a scientific basis. It is a basis on great ethical principles. It is not a series of conceptions deduced from another central conception or grouped round a favoured doctrine of a favourite Divine—a Calvinism, a Lutheranism, an Arminianism, or any conceivable ism. It is a grouping round law, spiritual, moral, natural law, a structure reared on the eternal order of the world, and therefore natural, self-evident, self-sustaining and invulnerable.

This method, dealing as it does with law and spirit, ignores nothing, denies nothing, and formally supplants nothing in the older subject-matter; but it tries to get deeper into the heart of it, and seeks a new life even in doctrines which seem to have long since petrified into stone. This was largely Christ's own method. He dealt with principles—His teaching was mainly excavation—the disinterring of hidden things, the bringing to light of the profound ethical principles hidden beneath Rabbinic subtleties and Pharisaic forms.

The Reformation—Protestantism—these were large attempts in the same direction, and modern thought is the heir to this spirit. Being a process of growth, and not a series of operations upon specific theological positions, this method is in the best sense constructive. It can never destroy except empty forms. To be negative, to oppose or denounce time-honoured doctrines is poor work—poor work which unfortunately many minds and pens and pulpits are continually trying to do. The only legitimate way to destroy an old doctrine is Christ's way to fulfil it. Instead of busying themselves about its death and calling their congregations ostentatiously to attend the funeral, the new theology will invite them rather to witness anew the resurrection of the undying spirit still hidden beneath the worn-out body of its older form.

As an illustration of what I mean, I propose to select one or two Christian doctrines which in their current forms have lost their power for thinking men, and try to show how these may live once more and play a powerful part in current teaching. One or two of the greatest Christian truths have already been so abundantly re-illuminated and re-spiritualised by modern literature and preaching that one need only name them. An admirable case is the doctrine of inspiration. It is idle to deny that the authority of the Bible was all but gone within this generation. The old view had become absolutely untenable, misleading and mischievous. But from the hands of reverent men who have studied the inward characters of these books, we have again got our Bible. The theory of development, the study of the Bible as a library of religious writings rather than as a book; the treatment of the writers as authors and not as pens; the mere discovery that religion has not come out of the Bible, but that the Bible has come out of religion: these announcements have not only destroyed with a breath a hundred infidel objections to Scripture, but opened up a world of new life and interest to Christian people.

So thoroughly has the spiritual as opposed to the mechanical theory of inspiration imbued all recent teaching that the battle for Scotland at least may be said to be now won. If there is anything further to be said on the subject, indeed, it is to caution ourselves against going too far or being very positive.

Modern criticism in this country, especially of the Old Testament, is not in a good way. The permission to embark upon it at all is sudden, and very few men are sufficiently equipped for a responsible reconstruction. Probably in Old Testament criticism there are not ten competent experts in the country, and these are all more or less disagreed, and what is more, afraid to announce their disagreements lest the others should turn and rend them. One of the greatest of these ten has just written an important book. I happen to know that it is being handed about among the nine for a review in a certain high-class theological monthly, and not a man of them will touch it.

Hasty conclusions as to authorship or canonicity are as foreign to the scientific spirit as the old dogmatism. Guinness Rogers has well pointed out that in the far future, when English has become a dead language, almost no internal evidence would allow the literary critic to allocate the authorship of John Gilpin, e.g., to the melancholy recluse who wrote the Olney hymns; and in dealing with questions of Biblical authorship the minute scholarship of this day, based on favourite words and particular styles of thought, is often in danger of ignoring such broader facts as the versatility of human nature, the changing moods of thinkers, the contradictions which Dr. Jekyll and Mr. Hyde exhibit within the same man's soul at the same period, or at contrasted periods of his life of which history can keep no cognisance.

This remark applies with even greater force to the subject-matter of the Books. We have treatises written, for instance, on the theology of Peter. Men talk of the Petrine conception of this and the Petrine presentation of that; they contrast the Petrine standpoint with the Pauline and the Johannine, and even go the length of fixing the proportion in which the various theological truths were held in the Petrine system. The absurdity of all this may be seen from a single fact. The entire Petrine remains that have come down to us and upon which all these elaborate structures are reared amount to a page or two, all that the apostle ever wrote or all that is left to us. They could be read to a congregation in exactly half the time that it would take a minister to deliver a half-hour's sermon. Think of the absurdity of judging a man's theology, or the proportion in which he held its various parts, by half a sermon, and you will never again hear the word Petrine without a smile. The men, and especially the Germans, who allow internal evidence—not seeing its excessive limitations—to be abused in this way are the true literalists, and their provincial analysis can only hinder the victory of a spiritual cause. If the new theology is the scientific spirit, that class of work is its stultification.

But to pass on to another instance. The unearthing of the tremendous ethical principle underlying the atonement is now restoring that central doctrine to theology just when in its mechanical forms it was on the point of being discredited by every thinking mind. The Salvation Army preacher, it is true, still preaches it as a syllogism, and pays the penalty in the utter apathy or mystification of his hearers at least on that point. But no man who preaches the spirit of it, instead of the phrases of it, will lose his audience. The man who makes words, even Bible words, the substitute for thought, can never be understood of the common people at the present day. There is nothing the street preacher needs to be warned against with more earnestness than the mechanical preaching of the syllogisms of the atonement. One listens often and with admiration and respect to the powerful way the street preacher brings home the great facts of personal sin to the crowd around him, to his almost melting appeal for instant decision to this offer of salvation—nearly always in my experience glowing with real enthusiasm and backed with an almost contagious faith and hope. But when he tries at that point to answer the simple inquiry, How? when he stands face to face with the question of the drunkard leaning against the lamp-post, "What must I, the drunkard, standing here to-night in Argyle Street, do to be saved?" he takes refuge in some text or metaphor, a proposition, and passes on. What I complain of in Gospel addresses is that many have no Gospel in them, no tangible thing for a drowning man to really see and clutch. They break down at the very point where they ought to be most strong and luminous. To tell the average wife-beater to take shelter behind the blood or to hide himself in the cleft is to put him off with a phrase. I do not object to these metaphors, I believe in metaphors. I go the length of holding that you never get nearer to truth than in a metaphor; but you have not told this man the whole truth about your metaphor, nor have you touched his soul or his affections with what lies beneath that metaphor; and it falls upon his ear as a tale he has heard a thousand times before. It is not obstinacy that keeps this poor man from religion—it is pure bewilderment as to what in the world we are driving at. The new theology when it preaches the atonement will not be less loyal to that doctrine, but more. It will not take refuge in the poor excuse for slipshod preaching and unthought-out doctrines that we must wait for God's light to break. God's light breaks through some men's preaching, through some clear, honest, convincing statement of truth, and not occultly. Faith cometh by hearing, and if our plan of salvation is not telling upon our audience it is blasphemy to blame God's spirit. The blame lies in our own spirit and in our offering words instead of spirit, and in our neglect to spend time and thought, in trying to get down to the professed meaning and omnipotent dynamic of the law of Sacrifice.

If a man has not something more to say about the atonement than the conventional phrases, let him be silent. By introducing from time to time he may earn the cheap reputation of being orthodox; but it is for him to consider whether that is an object for which his conscience will let him work. There are thousands of tender and conscientious souls now in our midst who cannot find that foothold on the conventional doctrine which they are led to believe their teachers have, and without which they feel themselves excommunicate from the work of the Church and the fold of Christ. If we see no further behind these words, let us say so, and not keep up this fraud, or preach these words, until we have sunk our spirits in them and can teach them with vital force and truth.

* * * * *

Gentlemen, I do not for a moment mean that we are to treat our congregations to dissertations on biology. Nature—human nature—are to be to us but discoveries of things as they are, the expression of principle, the theatre, on whose stupendous stage each can see with his own eyes the great laws act.

And this leads me to a final statement. We have seen that the method of the new Evangelism is to deal with principles. The mental act by which we are to search for truth, truth being in this spiritual form, is not therefore to be so much the reason, but the imagination. We are to put up truth when we deliver truth to others, not in the propositional form, but in some visual form—some form in which it will be seen without any attempt to prove. Truth never really requires to be proved. The best you can do for a law is to exhibit it.

Gentlemen, as a preparation for the work of the new Evangelism in which you are to spend your lives, I commend you to the study of the principles of the laws of God in nature, and in human nature: the development of that seeing power, as opposed to mere logic, which discerns the unseen through the seen. About the greatest thing a man can do, Ruskin tells us, is to see something, and tell others what he sees.

The Gospel as Christ gave it was a gift to the seeing power in man. His speech was almost wholly addressed to the imagination, to the imagination in its true sense, and this, which is the highest language of science, is also the language of poetry and of the poetry of the soul, which is religion. Unless we can fill the new theology with what the soul sees and feels, and sees to be true and feels to be living, it will be as juiceless and inert as the old dogmatic.

For it is only a living spirit of truth that can touch dead spirit, and the test of any theology is not that it is logically clear or even intellectually solid, but that it carries with it some sanctifying power.

These examples of the rejuvenescence of old truths under the more spiritual treatment of an ethical theology are more or less obvious. I wish in the time that remains to apply the method a little more in detail to one particular department of theology, which is perhaps less intruded upon by modern teachers. The revolt of the moral sense of this country against the doctrine of a physical hell, and the appeal to a Judgment Day, has lately led to almost complete silence on the whole subject of eschatology. Is this great theme or any part of it —say the conception of a Day of Judgment—not capable of a deeper ethical treatment? If the Divine judgment upon sin lies in the natural law of heredity, may we not find among the laws of the moral world some larger and more universal principle of judgment which shall restore the appeal of these forgotten dogmas to their place in religious teaching? It is quite clear we must discuss this or remain silent. No man can now say such words to his people as these—I quote from no less an authority than Jonathan Edwards,—"The God that holds you over the pit of Hell, much as one holds a spider or some loathsome insect over the fire, abhors you. It is nothing but His Hand that holds you from falling into the fire every moment; it is to be ascribed to nothing else that you did not go to Hell last night; and there is no other reason why you have not dropped into Hell since you arose in the morning. . . . There is nothing else to be given as a reason why you do not this very moment drop down into Hell."

That kind of thing is not over, though we may hear little of it.

Many of you have seen some, at least, of the great classical pictures of the Last Judgment. Here [in the next chapter] is Ruskin's account of the greatest of them all, the Last Judgment of Tintoretto, which hangs on a well-known church wall in Venice, in full view of the congregation.

Survival of the Fittest

Formed part of preceding address.

Perhaps the most weird picture in "Modern Painters" is the description of Tintoretto's "Last Judgment." Dante in poetry, Giotto, Orcagna, and Michael Angelo on canvas, have spent their imaginations on the unimaginable theme; but Tintoretto alone, says Mr. Ruskin, has grappled with this awful event in its verity: "Bat-like, out of the holes and caverns and shadows of the earth, the bones gather, and the clay-heaps heave, rattling and adhering into half-kneaded anatomies, that crawl and startle, and struggle up among the putrid weeds, with the clay clinging to their clotted hair, and their heavy eyes sealed with the earth darkness yet, like his of old who went his way unseeing to Siloam Pool; shaking off one by one the dreams of the prison-home, hardly hearing the clangour of the trumpets of the armies of God, blinded yet more, as they awake, by the white light of the new Heaven, until the great vortex of the four winds bears up their bodies to the judgment seat: the firmament is all full of them, a very dust of human souls, that drifts, and floats, and falls in the interminable, inevitable light; the bright clouds are darkened with them as with thick snow, currents of atom life in the arteries of heaven, now soaring up slowly, farther, and higher, and higher still, till the eye and the thought can follow no farther, borne up, wingless, by their inward faith and by the angel powers invisible, now hurled in countless drifts of horror before the breath of their condemnation." Such is the picture, "not typically nor symbolically," Mr. Ruskin tells us, "but as they may see it who shall not sleep, but be changed."

That artist and critic have drunk in the spirit of their dreadful subject may be unquestioned. That pictures of the Last Judgment, whether with pen or pigment, serve a certain function, is also beyond dispute. To deny this would be to condemn the whole of sacred art. And to have the mute appeal of the great religious masterpieces silenced in the thronged galleries of Europe, where they have stood like beacons to the passing stream of life for centuries, would be a blow to Christianity. But it is no less true that to a class of minds the dramatic aspects of the Last Judgment appeal in vain. The material imagery, we are assured, the marshalling of the prisoners at the trumpet call, the Judge and the great White Throne, are presentations to an age which has passed away. The very tying-down of Judgment to a Day, the whole machinery of a human court "which meets, goes through its docket and adjourns," are out of harmony with the other ways of God; and whatever reality may underlie it, the conception, as it stands at present, is too gross and artificial to find acceptance with a scientific age.

Many will wonder what science means by this fastidiousness. Some will quite fail even to enter into the state of mind which feels it, or which presumes to question the congruity or incongruity of what has been revealed. Nevertheless, this is a real difficulty. And, whatever be its genesis, we are compelled to recognise an attitude of mind which somehow disqualifies its possessor from being greatly influenced by such spectacular representations as have been named. Our feelings are a great mystery; the least definable are often those which sway us most. But to meet this state of mind, rather than to defend its reasonableness or ban its presumption, is the question before us. For the difficulty, after giving up a truth in one form, of winning it back in another is very great. And it is certainly true that for want of a connecting link between the popular doctrines of eschatology, and the facts and ways of nature and of the moral life, many who in this instance have repudiated the form have come to abandon the substance. To restore the substance and meaning of the idea of judgment by seeking to renovate the form is our object now. We are far from claiming that the form to be presented is the best, still less that it contains the whole of the substance. Truth has many forms, and the whole substance of this truth is, perhaps, not given as yet to man to know. But upon this, the most solemn thought that has ever been presented to the conscience of mankind, it is impossible that reason should be silent, or nature withhold its contribution from such a theme.

We have hinted that the scientific difficulty in accepting the doctrine in its conventional form is one of standpoint. But the particular point of the objection is worth defining, and for a remarkable reason. What science really rebels at in the old doctrine is its externalness. It is outside nature, a foreign and unanticipated element, a breach of continuity. And what science would like to see is a universal principle, a principle, if possible, operating from within, bound up with nature itself, and involved in the general system of things. Now, such a claim coming from science is in every way astonishing and unexpected. For observe what it is. It is simply a demand upon religion for a further spirituality. It is really materialism that science objects to in the old doctrine—it objects to a material throne, and bar, and trumpet, to an external law, to a judgment from without rather than from within. The protest, in fact, is a rebuke to religion for the grossness of its conceptions, for its tardy abandonment of the letter, for the permanence it has given to provisional forms—in short, for its unspirituality.

Nor is this the first instance in which science has called the attention of religion to this crude externaless in its ideas. In several well-known instances it has already imposed upon religion the useful task of remodelling its doctrines; and in each case the gain has been in the direction of greater inwardness, greater naturalness, greater spirituality. And the still more interesting fact remains to be noted, that it is generally science itself which supplies the material for the remodelled doctrine. As it destroys, it fulfils—the very discoveries which begat its doubt become, when rearranged and incorporated by religion, the materials for a firmer faith. For instance, the grossness and externalness of the old theory of a Six Days' Creation was once a serious stumbling-block to science. Students of nature were unaccustomed to find nature working in ways so abrupt; facts proving the slow development of the world had accumulated; the Divine-fiat hypothesis was challenged, and finally abandoned. And then out of these very facts grew the new and beautiful theory that Creation was not a stupendous and catastrophic operation performed from without, but a silent process acting from within. So, having destroyed the old conception, science itself contributed the new—a conception which it could not only intelligently accept, but which for religion also left everything more worthy of worship than before.

Again, consider a case where the difficulty of believing an accepted theory is not physical but moral. Take the second commandment. The impression this law would leave on the early mind would certainly be that, in visiting the iniquities of fathers upon children, God weighed each case separately and administered special judgment upon cases of exceptional enormity. God administered punishment, that is to say, from without, by judicial enactments, augmenting or remitting sentence according to discretion. But instead of referring the enforcement of this commandment to an external court, we now see that execution of its sentences are transferred to the laws of nature. Instead of working from without, from above nature, it works, in ordinary circumstances at least, within it. It is, in fact, the ordinary law of heredity—the law of transmission from sire to son of the dispositions, tendencies, temptations, and diseases of the parent. Now, while losing nothing here, much is gained. The idea of judgment for sin is as much in the law as ever, the personality of the Judge is as before; but the seat of judgment has changed, and the mechanism of justice is replaced by the working of inherent laws. The very laws of nature have become "the hands of the living God."

Now with these two examples before us of the change of emphasis from the external to the internal, may we not ask whether any parallel change is warranted in the case of the larger doctrine now in view? Should it not also have an inward ground, a discoverable law? Is it an operation from without, or a process from within? Is there no anticipation, in short, in nature of a final judgment? As it is not intended to deal here directly with the Scripture references, I will leave them with two remarks.

1. The Scriptures are not explicit—are, in fact, very far from explicit. Let any one collate the various references to this subject—and they are very numerous—sift them with whatever care he likes, arrange them upon whatever principle he likes, or upon all known principles of interpretation up to the present time, and he will find them perplexing, and even contradictory. Here, if anywhere then, there is room for the New Testament to come in and seek out a basis of law. And I select the field as an illustration, simply because it is a remote one, and at the first blush most unpromising.

2. That while Christ lays down, and especially in the parables of Judgment, the great ethical principles of eschatology, nearly all beyond that, in His teaching and in Paul's, has a purely Jewish or Rabbinic basis. No theme is more prominent in Jewish literature. The older portions of the book of Enoch, for example, contain constant allusions to a "Great Judgment," "the Day of the Great Judgment," "the Great Day of Judgment," "the Great Day," "the Day of Judgment," "the Righteous Judgment," and "the Last Judgment for all Eternity." The Sibylline books and the Apocalypses generally teem with detailed descriptions of such an event variously conceived of, variously dated, and for the most part having a political origin and significance. "Even the idea of `a day` (according to Stanton) does not seem to have been originally taken from a judge holding court, but from a terrible triumphal conqueror executing vengeance in a day of battle and slaughter."

But to proceed. The position to be now taken up is not only the one which will be obvious on a little thought—that Judgment is not an act to be accomplished, an act sudden, spectacular, explosive, but a quiet process now and ever going on— but that that process is simply the operation of one of the widest and most familiar of the Laws of Nature.

This law let me first bring forward in its simplicity as mere natural law; later on, we shall reach its ethical relations; and I must be pardoned for speaking here my own native tongue of Science rather than attempting a translation into ethics. The name of this law is the Survival of the Fittest. Eternal life under the last analysis is a question of the survival of the fittest. And Judgment is a question of natural selection. In spite of the constantly reiterated protest of popular theology that science and religion part company for ever over this law, in spite of the apparent objection that while in nature the prize is to the strong, and the weak go to the wall, in the kingdom of grace the bruised reed is not broken and the weary and heavy laden win; it is the most certain of truths that in nature and grace alike the law of the survival of the fittest holds. A moment's reflection will show that in thus contrasting the genius of nature and the genius of Christianity by way of objection, the word fitness is used in two totally different senses. In the one case it is employed in a biological, in the other in an ethical sense. When it is said that a fish survives in water because it is "fit" for it, all that is meant is that the organization of the fish is, in certain respects, adapted for this element. And when it is said that eternal life is a question of the survival of the fittest, what is implied is that it is a question of the survival of the adapted—of those who, by some means, have become specially fitted or equipped for living in this element. In this—the only possible scientific sense—it is literally and eternally true that the future state is a question of the survival of the fittest. The survival of the fittest means, then, only the survival of the adapted. It is not asserted, meantime, that the survival of the adapted means also the survival of the worthiest. Whether worthiness be, after all, the same thing as fitness will be referred to presently. But that no moral quality whatever is involved in the operation of this law is a point to be marked, for the basis of judgment for which we contend is one involved in the very constitution of the world.

The essential thing in any organism in relation to its surroundings, the characteristic quality on which life depends, is adaptation to environment. If an organism is to survive in water, it must be adapted to the aquatic condition by the development of a water breathing faculty, a gill. If it is to change its surroundings so as to live in air—as actually happens during the life-history of the common frog—it must become adapted to correspond with the atmosphere by the development of an air-breathing apparatus, or lung. So if the highest organism is to be in correspondence with the Divine Environment, he must be adapted to it. He, the Christian, must have undergone some process of adaptation to environment—theologically called sanctification—in virtue of which he is able to correspond, to commune, with God. Only those so adapted can possibly exist in this element, even as those only equipped with gill can breathe in water, or those with lung in air. But this is simply to repeat once more that the adapted survive; that the fit survive; that they are "selected" to live by the possession of the required faculty.

Suppose, now, to point the application, these varying degrees of adaptation to environment to be tested by actual experiment. A pool teeming with living organisms suddenly dries up. The vast majority of these organisms are adapted for an aquatic environment and for no other, and with the removal of this they perish. In terms of adaptation to environment they are judged. One or two, however, such as the water-newt, in addition to the special adaptation required for the liquid element possess the further power of corresponding with the earth and air in virtue of the possession of a lung. So long, therefore, as it can remain in correspondence with the earth and air, it lives. Suppose next some climatic change to occur, or some physical catastrophe such as the sudden eruption of a volcano, and that those who escaped from the water are no longer able to adapt themselves to this further change. In terms of environment they are judged. Suppose, however, that another organism, man, within the affected area was able to escape. His survival is due solely to the superior complexity of his organization. By his intelligence he foretold the calamity, and prepared for it, or with the aid of his inventions he swiftly withdrew to a safe distance. But suppose next, by a mightier catastrophe, the earth itself should collide with another star, and make his new environment again untenable. What is to become of him? It will depend on what correspondences remain, and on what environment still exists. But the old law holds He will go where he is fit for, and be in what is fit for him. If he has any correspondence with eternity, he will go on living in terms of these correspondences.

He will go on living in terms of his correspondences—this is the point of it all. And this is natural selection; it is another way of saying that the fit to survive survive. And is there not here a principle of Judgment? The organisms in the drying pool, the water-newt upon the quaking land, the man at the world's collapse—each is allocated to his place according to his correspondences. No external act of choice takes place; there is an inherent claim to live, or an inherent necessity to die, in the organism itself This claim is founded on the fulfilment or non-fulfilment of an essential and imperative condition; it is a necessary consequence of the law of the survival of the fittest; it is not an arbitrary appointment or reward, it is the natural evolution of an organism in terms of its correspondences.

Nature sits upon no far-off throne, like a capricious goddess, signalling which shall live and which shall die. But in the very inmost being of each she discloses a law of life or death. If an animal dies, its death is the natural culmination of its own past, of tendencies, proclivities, and processes already at work within; if it lives, its survival is the direct result of what it at the moment is. If death is, in such cases, in any sense a judgment, it is a judgment solely on unfitness. And if in dissolution the sentence of a judge is being carried out, it is not by an external operation, but by an inward process. And so with man. It is not necessary that he should be judged from without; he will be judged from within. He is his own judge.

No witnesses need be called to give their evidence; the witnesses are himself. No gaolers need be told off to watch him; he cannot run away from himself. No external court need formulate the case against him; his own past has done it, his own past is it. No Judge need pronounce sentence at a Last Day; as he stands there to-day, he has sentenced himself,—as he stands there, he is prisoner, gaoler, court, witnesses, all in one, all the past collected and focussed in his present, all the present defining and determining the unknown, but not unanticipated, future. As in the past evolution of the earth the nebulous gases combined in the order of their affinities and arranged themselves in the order of their densities, so in the future evolution will each go to his own, living on in terms of his correspondences, in the order determined by his spiritual affinities.

This principle of judgment pervades with its invisible presence the whole of nature. Every plant, insect, animal, man—man physical, mental, moral, spiritual—is daily and hourly on trial. This court is never opened and never closed. It is a vast, mysterious, self-acting organization, ramifying through the whole of nature, and without resistance or appeal, each living thing obeys its verdict.

But, in the case of an organism, what is it that betrays the insufficiency of its correspondences? It is the presentation to it of the new environment. So long as the fish lives in the stream, it will neither feel nor exhibit any want of adaptation to other surroundings. But when the stream runs dry? So long as the swallow lives in the English climate, its joyful existence is complete. But when the English summer wanes and the chills of winter come? So long as man lives on in the environment of this present world, his correspondences, or some of them, are satisfied. But when this present world is done? Then is the great trial. Then is the sifting time. Then is the Judgment Day. Then his sufficiency or insufficiency is finally betrayed. In presence of the new environment—not by any book opened, word spoken, past recalled—in the mere presence of it, he is made manifest. This reflex influence of environment has been a commonplace with theology from the beginning. It is remarkable how full revelation is of this still future truth—remarkable also that, being a thing to come, nature should so anticipate and confirm it. No thought is more frequent or more solemn in the Biblical accounts of the last things than that at the appearing of Christ a mighty change will sweep over the moral world—a sudden revolution in men's opinions—a swift reversal of all human judgments. And this is not an unlooked-for crisis. It is the natural effect of the new environment—or of the sudden prominence of the new environment—upon organisms well or ill prepared to live in it. Hence it is not only that in this Presence the secrets of all hearts shall be revealed, nor that human lives projected against His will henceforth and evermore appear in colours black as hell. But it will be that vital relations will manifest themselves in the case of every man; his correspondences will continue, or come short. All that he is, the little that he is, all that he is fit for, all that he is not fit for, will be revealed. In terms of these, in himself, and at a glance, he will know whether he is to live or die. With his own eyes he will see the great gulf fixed; with his own reason he will see why it cannot be crossed

"The appearing of Christ," says Van Oosterzee, "brings about separation (krisi) between the one who has the Son and the one who has Him not; or rather, the difference, already present, unseen, is in consequence of His coming and His work, brought to light. Thus the Christ becomes necessarily Judge, even where He desires to be Saviour." And to the same effect Paul, "For we must all be made manifest before the Judgment-seat of Christ." This is that being "weighed in the balance" in which some shall be "found wanting." This is what Paul foresaw when he said, "We must all be made manifest before the Judgment-seat of Christ."

This, again, is not peculiar to Christianity or to science, but universal law. The moment I go to a high-class concert, in the matter of musical taste I am judged. My musical soul, or soul-lessness, is instantly made manifest. The moment I enter a picture gallery I am judged. My correspondences are or are not. I am weighed in the balances. That day declares it.

What man is what God is—these are the materials for the anticipation of judgment. They are in each man's hands, and in terms of them he can here and now decide. To no man, surely, is it ever given to draw aside the veil and forecast the future for another. Personal to the individual, the possession of the appropriate correspondences,—the adaptation to the Divine is truly known to oneself alone. And we are therefore warned by the New Testament: "Judge nothing before the time, 'until the Lord come,' who both will bring to light the hidden things of darkness, and will make manifest the counsels of the heart." But so far from precluding a judgment of our own upon ourselves, the very inability of our neighbour, the impotence to help of those who know and love us best, the isolation and solitude in which we must settle this question of life and death, create a warrant for self-examination such as no serious man will allow himself to evade. "Examine yourselves," says Paul, "whether ye be in the faith; prove your own selves." And again, "Make your calling and election sure."

* * * *

Mr. Darwin tells us that the object of natural selection—the object of the fittest surviving—is "the improvement of organisms." It is the means by which nature shows her appreciation, not of fitness alone, but of fitness in the direction of advancement. It is her splendid effort to ennoble life, to exalt and purify creation, to bring all organisms to an ever-increasing perfectness and complexity, to carry on the evolution of the world to higher and higher beauty, usefulness, and efficacy. How keen her desire to compass this great end, how enormous the value she sets on the result, may be feebly inferred from the terrible price she is prepared to pay for it. If nature is in earnest about one thing, it is quality. To this end all her labour tends; she works, and waits; she destroys, and re-creates. And surely nothing is more significant for religion, nothing could more eloquently express its own deepest aim for the world, than this mighty gravitation of all in nature towards fitness, wholeness, perfectness. Even Lamarck finds himself so impressed by the silent witnesses around him to the great ascent of life as to believe in "an innate and inevitable tendency towards perfection in all organic beings."

But it is to the various eschatological theories of theology that its voice most distinctly speaks. Has Antinomianism no tacit following in the modern Church? Let those who have to meet this subtle and monstrous and unaccountable perversion explain the meaning and press home the necessity of adaptation to environment. Let it be shown that fitness to survive is tested, not by profession, but by experiment. How easily in the theological forms may faith be a correspondence, a communion, a living bond with a living Christ, or (it may be) a mere belief, a barren formula, a name to live. There is an ecclesiastical Christ and a living Christ; there is a historical Christ and a risen Christ; there is a theological Christ and a personal Christ. Is it not clear alike from reason from nature, and from revelation that only by contact—immediate, personal, living—with a living, present Christ the eternal life can be a root in the heart of man? We turn to yet another tendency of the time. More and more the doctrines of Universalism seem to spread.

Where then, it may be asked, is mercy? The answer is—(1) It will be seen presently that the whole scheme is established only in mercy; but (2) even mercy has its laws. The object of mercy can never be to "save" the unfit, i.e. to save the unadapted, which is inconceivable and impossible. Mercy can make the unfit fit; it has a vast machinery for this one purpose. That is its work, its line, the only line it can take. To "fit" the unfit is a possibility, to "save" them being unfit, to sentence them unfit in either relation to a heaven or a hell is impossible. The only conceivable ways to save a fish tossed on the rocks by a billow are to suddenly supply it with a lung, which is impossible, or to turn it back into its own element. On similar principles the unfit in relation to God cannot be saved, the fit can by no possibility be lost.

As the evangelist said of Emerson, "Emerson was one of the most beautiful souls I ever knew. There is something wrong with his machinery somewhere, but I do not know what it is, for I never heard it jar. He cannot be lost, for if he went to hell, the devil would not know what to do with him."

* * * * *

But we must shape this many-sided inquiry to a close.

One other aspect of this Truth demands a passing notice before we close. Till now we have discussed the survival of the fittest only as it affects the individual. This is a small part of the truth. No law is of private interpretation. How calmly we, as individuals, appropriate the laws of God focussing all in our own little world—as if they were only for ourselves; as if they were not the parallel of latitude of a larger universe, the revelation of the method of God's whole purposes and government. What is each man but one little thread in the loom of God? The great wheels revolve, the shuttle flies, not for the thread but for the web; not for the web alone, but for the pattern on the web; not for the pattern on the web, but for One, the Designer, who makes loom and web and pattern for Himself. To know why the loom is there, and why the shuttle moves, and why the threads are in this place or in that, or why they are there at all, we must look beyond ourselves, discover if we may the hidden Workman's purpose, and see in the half-finished design the prophecy of some final harmony.

Revelation is too prophetic of the End, and creation is too full of God and of His plans to leave man without a clue to the larger meanings of the natural laws. In the natural world the function of the law of the survival of the fittest is to produce fitness—to make a select world (a cosmos, beautiful, harmonious) perfect. So is it in the spiritual world. There its function will surely be to secure and guarantee the quality of the Kingdom of God.

If it is necessary that there should be a heaven, it is necessary that it should be kept heavenly. This is that law which now and evermore keeps heaven pure. It has more than a personal application; it is a chief factor in the great evolution, one of the main instruments by which nature passes on to these nobler and nobler developments in which all changes, forces, and movements in nature appear to be culminating. So far as science can read the secret will and purpose of creation, it is this, that Nature is gravitating with infinite patience and sureness towards perfection.

The object of the Law of the Survival of the fittest is to produce fitness. And this is the object of Judgment—to produce fitness here by the terror of its law hereafter, to separate the chaff from the wheat, yet not for the sake of punishing the chaff, only for the sake of preserving the wheat. This is the great law whose secret operations tend to make a select world. It is the guarantee of the quality of the Kingdom of God.

Even now, in some poor way, we seem to see how God proceeds to secure His end. Our little world has had its own life-history. In the life-history of this one world we can dimly make out, not only the direction, but the method of progress, for every feature in its marvellous evolution is a further vision of things to come. Look into this past for a moment, observe God's way of producing earth from chaos, and say whether no clue lies here to that further evolution of heaven from earth.

The Third Kingdom

[The introductory page of the MS., which is lost, doubtless contained a reference to a division into Inorganic or First Kingdom, Organic or Second, and Spiritual or Third.]

I may be permitted to summarize briefly the teaching of the Sacred Books on the central subject of the Kingdom of God, and to point it, as occasion may offer, with reference to the present inquiry.

The Kingdom of God the Central Idea of the Old and New Testaments

That God was preparing out of the Second Kingdom a people for Himself is the most prominent fact of ancient history. For centuries the children of Israel were so impressed with this belief that they dared not, like other nations, permit themselves even to own an earthly king. With Jehovah to defend their case, with the King of kings to define and carry out their cause, generation after generation held out against the temptation to create a human monarchy, and handed down unsoiled to the late age of the Captivity their theocratic faith. "The dominating thought of the Old Testament," to quote the words of Keim, "is that of the Kingdom of God upon earth. God is the God, the Lord, the King of the whole earth; but from among all the nations He has chosen Israel to be His peculiar possession, His servants, His people, His firstborn, His priestly kingdom. God is Israel's King, and rules as King. God fulfils His regal office by spiritually and physically bringing the nation into existence; by protecting, regulating, and guiding it with His blessings and His chastisements. He does all this, sometimes by His immediate presence, and sometimes through the agency of His inspired organs—lawgivers and generals, priests and prophets, and finally kings, who, in fact, are only viceroys. This kingdom has, however, its limits; the nations without do not obey, they make attacks upon the people of God, and the people of God sin against themselves and against their King."

How a thousand years before the birth of Christ the longing rose for the Kingdom of God in a more perfect form, for a Kingdom that should conquer and rule the nations and establish righteousness and peace on earth; how, fostered by the startling assurances of Daniel, the desire was kept alive through ages of oppression, and burned only the more clearly after prolonged disappointment; how centuries after the voice of prophecy was silent in their land, when the Forerunner raised his standard in the wilderness, the old hope, deeper still in their hearts than any thought of God or man, uttered itself again in an almost national response to the Baptist's message—these points have but to be named to convince us of the thrilling reality of the Kingdom of God to the ancient Jewish Church.

To point out the development of the conception as we come down to New Testament times is all but superfluous. At the double risk of appearing to the world as an imitator of John, and to the Roman as sharing with the Baptist the responsibilities of political revolution, Jesus accepted the watchword of the hour and deliberately announced Himself as the King of the promised Kingdom. How He gathered about Him the first few subjects, and in the face of laughter and blasphemy assumed the Sovereignty of the miniature State, framing a Constitution for it as far-reaching and profound as if it were already a great nation, is a plain fact of history. And as one follows His life throughout, it is patent to the most casual reader of the Gospel narratives that His one idea was to found on earth the Kingdom of Heaven. In Matthew alone the expressions "Kingdom of Heaven" and "Kingdom of God" occur forty-five times; and generally the theme seems never to have been absent for a single hour from the thoughts of Jesus during His earthly ministry. "In the contemplation of the doctrine of the Lord," says Van Oosterzee, "according to the Synoptics, we must proceed from the foundation-thought by which, above all others, it is ruled. It is that of the Kingdom of God." So Reuss, "L'idee fondamentale, qui se reproduit a chaque instant dans l'enseignement de Jesus, est celle du royaume de Dieu."

Were an evolutionist asked to formulate the fundamental idea of nature, he would reply, in the light of all modern philosophy and science, The idea of the Kingdom. All nature, he would say, is gravitating towards a nobler order of things. The vision of the past presents man with a grand and harmonious picture of the Ascent of Life. Kingdom is seen to be rising above kingdom. And yet withal the apex of the pyramid is still concealed. The perfect is not yet come. The whole creation groaneth and travaileth, waiting for the redemption of the creature. Scarce less audible is the prophecy of nature than the voice of Old Testament Scripture as to the coming of the world's Redeemer. And Science, like the Forerunner of the Messiah, has prepared the way of the Lord.

The Object of the Third Kingdom

What is the ultimate purpose of God in the further evolution of man can only be dimly discerned. With words, it is true, we can fill in logically the framework; of the future; but to the imagination, beyond a certain point, these words become colourless symbols of a reality which man in this life can never grasp. Still it is not denied us to see a little way into the Third

Kingdom, and we may attempt at least a provisional answer to this question, What does the Kingdom of God propose to do for mankind?

The form of the question which chiefly interests us in the present inquiry is, Does the Kingdom of God propose to do anything abnormal, extravagant, or unintelligible? Is it a new and unrelated effect that is to be wrought on the subjects of this Kingdom, or is it something still consistently in line with continuity? Certainly if it could be shown that the aim of the Third Kingdom was in harmony with all that has gone before, it would go a long way to remove any prejudice that may exist against it on the ground of what men call its unnaturalness and "other-worldliness."

The simplest method of testing the naturalness of the object of the Third Kingdom is to refer to the aim of the Second. What is it that serious men propose to themselves as the object of life? Is there not something that all have willed to achieve—a summum bonum—a chief end of man? These, for ages, have been the questions of philosophy. The greatest and wisest among mankind have studied this problem. And it would be idle to deny that their labours have achieved at least a general result. Without referring to any of the specific plans of life proposed by different schools, it will sufficiently summarize the conclusion of all to say that the highest aims of mankind are connected with the moral development of the race. Whatever methods various philosophies have pointed out in order to attain this end, and whatever shades of difference exist as to the end itself, there is no debate as to this general result. There is no question likewise, and this is an important consideration, that the ideal of philosophy has never yet been reached. With greater or less hope some philosophic schools still expect a future success to justify the principles they teach; others found wanting after fair trial have already withdrawn from the field. Still a unanimous consensus among men that the highest development of the race is the summum bonum is a fact too significant to be ignored. And any new applicant for favour might be expected beforehand to enter the field with this same general aim in spite of the warnings of those who have failed. Any other aim would be unnatural.

Now as a matter of fact the aim of Christianity, in its general direction, is the aim of all philosophy. Christianity fell naturally into the stream of evolution which was carrying the world through kingdom after kingdom to a high and perfect development. Its idea of development was immeasurably loftier than that of philosophy, and the means for carrying out the process were altogether different; but the goal in either case, though not the same, lay in the same general line. I have defined the aim of philosophy to be the moral development of the race. When it is said, however, that this is also the aim of Christianity we must attach a higher significance to the term moral. Morality is a word of the Second Kingdom. In the Third we look for its evolution. We shall still recognise the old quality, but it will really exist in a form so greatly developed that we may be justified in substituting for morality the word spirituality. At the same time it must again be repeated that the development of the spiritual from the natural man is not a case of simple evolution. The natural character does not simply grow better and better until a pitch of excellence is reached such as finally deserves the distinguishing name of spirituality. Spirituality and morality differ qualitatively as well as quantitatively. The natural development can never pass the barrier separating the Second from the Third Kingdom. The transition is secured, just as in the case of atoms passing from the First to the Second Kingdom, by means of something not inherent in the lower Kingdom but communicated ab extra.

But while giving the fullest prominence to this cardinal fact that the spiritual is not a mere natural development of the natural, it is no less necessary to point out, although at first sight it seems a paradox, that the spiritual character is still a development of the natural. The first object of the Third Kingdom cannot, without misconception, be said to be the creating merely of a spiritual character. Its first work is to make what would be called a perfect natural character. It does not leave the Second Kingdom in a raw, unfinished state, and, regardless of the natural man, proceed to start afresh with a new set of organisms developing under a new regime. Its first business is to complete the old. It takes up a human life at the point where the natural world has left it and carries it on to perfection. There is, it is true, a new creature born within the natural man. And in this sense there is a new creation and a new departure. But the first work of the new nature is to operate on the old and do for it what it failed to do for itself. Thus the aim of the spiritual Kingdom in the first instance is to perfect the natural. The first object of Christianity is to make men. So far from being a dehumanizing process, it alone creates the true humanity. For the Third Kingdom alone possesses the true ideal, and alone contains the energies effectually to overpower those forces of sin which prevent men from ever becoming men.

I purposely refrain from making more than the most meagre allusion to the aims of the spiritual world, for the subject does not come directly within the biological province. Words at all times fail, however, to express the magnificence of the scheme of Christianity. For the past its provision is so complete, for the present so wonderful, for the future so glorious that the more one exercises his mind upon the religion of Jesus Christ the more is he impressed with its wisdom, magnificence, and thorough practical adaptation to every need and wish of man. The whole conception of the Redemption of the world. the amazing series of events projected in order to it, the possibility opened to man of a pure life and a disinterested deed, the promise of having all the haunting problems of life and time, all the soul's deep difficulties concerning the universe and the eternal finally solved—these alone mark out the Third Kingdom as a creation of the Most High. Nothing could be more exquisite than the programme of Christianity penned by Isaiah centuries before the Founder of the Kingdom was born in Bethlehem. One would come

"To preach good tidings to the meek;
To bind up the broken-hearted;
To proclaim liberty to the captives;
To comfort all that mourn;
To give unto them beauty for ashes,
The oil of joy for mourning,

The garment of praise for the spirit of heaviness;
That they might be called trees of righteousness, the planting of the Lord,
That He might be glorified."

Side by side with these words let him who would rate the claims of the Third Kingdom on his acceptance—unobtrusive claims which have always depended most on a mute appeal to their inherent dignity and grace—read the Sermon on the Mount. And if he would understand the aspirations of the Kingdom he will find the seven deepest thoughts of his own heart at its purest moments reflected in the seven petitions of the Lord's Prayer.

If that programme is not a satire on the gospels of humanity, if these Beatitudes are not a fiction, if the Lord's Prayer is not the expression of a need that is rarely felt and never gratified, they have a claim upon mankind more vitally real than anything else in the world. If there be a Kingdom of God, that programme, that Sermon and that Prayer are worthy of it. And if they be but a dream, I know not how we shall account for such a dream.

While the design of the Third Kingdom coincides somewhat with the purpose of Moral Philosophy, its apparatus and methods are widely different. And they are different mainly in respect of two things already mentioned. Christianity provides an ideal which is the highest possible, and equips the subjects of the Kingdom with powers in every way adequate to realize that ideal. The problems connected with the ideal will be referred to again, but the question of the powers of the spiritual Kingdom may now be dealt with under a separate head.

The Powers of the Third Kingdom

The fundamental difference between the Second and Third Kingdoms consists in what, for want of a better name, may be called their Energies. The difference of phenomena entirely depends on this—the difference, for example, between morality and spirituality. Philosophy may easily borrow the ideal from Christianity; to some extent it may attempt to introduce its motive, but it utterly breaks down in the practical application. And it fails for want of the one thing which finally differentiates the Third Kingdom from the Second—Life. Discussing Christianity on the philosophical plane in a chapter of singular insight and beauty, "Ecce Homo," while insisting upon the difference between Christianity and Moral Philosophy, fails withal, as it seems to me, to recognise the infinite and radical distinction between them, owing to a disregard of this unique quality of Life. "Philosophers had drawn their pupils from the elite of humanity; but Christ finds His material among the worst and meanest, for He does not propose merely to make the good better, but the bad good. And what is His machinery? He says the first step towards good dispositions is for a man to form a strong personal attachment. Let him first be drawn out of himself. Next, let the object of that attachment be a person of striking and conspicuous goodness. To worship such a person will be the best exercise in virtue that he can have. Let him vow obedience in life and death to such a person; let him mix and live with others who have made the same vow. He will have ever before his eyes an ideal of what he may himself become. His heart will be stirred by new feelings, a new world will be gradually revealed to him, and, more than this, a new self within his old self will make its presence felt, and a change will pass over him which he will feel it most appropriate to call a new birth." The fatal objection to this scheme is that it begins at the wrong end. Certain changes pass over a man's character; he forms a personal attachment, worships his ideal, learns obedience, and all this he will "feel it most appropriate" to call a new birth. Why not begin with the new birth? Why be guilty, even in appearance, of the scientific heresy of making Life the result of organization instead of the cause of it? The language used certainly lends itself at least to the supposition that the expression "new birth" is merely a metaphor—an "appropriate" term for the act after the result has appeared. And the criticism of "Ecce Homo" on Christianity in this respect is not exceptional, but representative. The Kingdom of Heaven is simply the "Society of Jesus," or "a religious-moral institution" (Van Oosterzee), or "a filial relation to God" (Hausrath).

Now, the Kingdom of God is all this, but it is also a great deal more. From the philosophical standpoint no definitions, probably, could be more exact; none other even are possible. But there has been a universal failure to regard the whole subject, in the first instance, as a question of Biology. Even those theologies which have recognised most clearly the special factor of Life in Christianity have still felt themselves insensibly drawn to discuss the question ultimately in terms of philosophy. That it is susceptible of philosophic treatment is abundantly plain; but it cannot with too much emphasis be pointed out that, alike from the analogies of nature and from the explicit declarations of its Founder, the Third Kingdom must be treated primarily as a biological question. Christ affirmed that His first object in coming to men was to give them Life—more abundant Life. And that He meant literal Life, literal spiritual Life, is clear from the whole course of His teaching and acting. To impose a metaphorical meaning on the commonest word of the New Testament is to violate every canon of interpretation, and at the same time to charge the greatest of Teachers with persistently mystifying His hearers by an unusual use of so exact a vehicle for expressing definite thought as the Greek language, on the most momentous subject of which He ever spoke—a subject, indeed, of life or death to all whom He addressed. It is a canon of interpretation, says Alford, that "a figurative sense of words is never admissible except when required by the context." The context in most cases is not only directly unfavourable to the figurative meaning, but in innumerable cases Life is broadly contrasted with Death. In others, as in the discourse with Nicodemus, the language used makes it inconceivable that there, at least, the symbolical meaning is implied. "Ye must be born again," said Jesus to the Rabbi. And that the words were taken literally is apparent from the answer: "How can a man be born when he is old? Can he enter a second time into his mother's womb and be born?" While undeceiving His pupil as to the acceptance of the term Life in its natural organic sense, Christ continues to insist withal that it is nevertheless Life—a deeper and spiritual Life, a Life mysteriously entering into the soul as by a breath from God. "Except a man be born of water and of the Spirit, he cannot enter into the Kingdom of God. . . . That which is born of the flesh is flesh, and that which is born of the spirit is spirit."

To pass from Christ's words to the teaching of the Apostles, we find that without exception they have accepted the term in its simple, literal sense. Reuss defines the Apostolic belief, as is his wont, with rigid impartiality when he discovers in the Apostles' conception of Life, first, "the idea of a real existence, an existence such as is proper to God and to the word; an imperishable existence—that is to say, not subject to the vicissitudes and imperfections of the finite world. This primary idea is repeatedly expressed, at least in a negative form; it leads to a doctrine of immortality, or, to speak more correctly, of life, far surpassing any that had been expressed in the formulas of the current philosophy or theology, and resting upon premises and conceptions altogether different. In fact, it can dispense both with the philosophical thesis of the immateriality or indestructibility of the human soul, and with the theological thesis of a miraculous corporeal reconstruction of our person: theses, the first of which is altogether foreign to the religion of the Bible, and the second absolutely opposed to reason" Second, "the idea of life, as it is conceived in this system, implies the idea of a power, an operation, a communication, since this life no longer remains, so to speak, latent or passive in God and in the Word, but through them reaches the believer. It is not a neutral, somnolent thing; it is not a plant without fruit; it is a germ which is to find fullest development."

The sum of New Testament doctrine is that there is an immediate action of the Spirit of God on the souls of men. In the New Testament alone the Spirit is referred to nearly three hundred times. And the one word with which He is constantly associated is Power. If we are asked to define more clearly what is meant by this Power we hand over the difficulty to science. When science can define Life and Force we may hope for further clearness on the nature and action of the Spiritual Powers. At the same time we are forewarned that with our present faculties we can never pass far beyond the threshold of these hidden things. Their very power of evading the senses is the mysterious token of their spirituality. It is the test of the Spirit that thou canst not tell whence it cometh or whither it goeth. If we could tell, if we could trace it naturally to its source, if we could account for its operations on ordinary principles, if we could define regeneration as the effect of moral persuasion, we should be dealing not with the Unknown but with the Known. It is from the analysis of natural religion, where the elements can all be rationally accounted for, that men derive their chief argument against the supernatural. But in analyzing spirituality the effort to detect the Living Spirit is as idle as to subject protoplasm to microscopic examination in the hope of discovering Life. When the Spiritual Life is discovered in the laboratory it will be time to give it up altogether. It may then say, as Socrates of his soul, "You can bury me—if you can catch me."

While the Powers of the Third Kingdom evade analysis their Energy is not less real. The activities of the Third Person of the Trinity have always been described as dynamical. The Spirit is the executive of the Godhead, carrying out the sovereign Will by operations as irresistible as they are subtle. To this omnipotent agency are to be referred ultimately all changes which take place within the Kingdom of God on earth. This is the Source of Energy for the Third Kingdom. And long before the days of Dynamics, when the energies of the Second Kingdom were less understood than now are those of the Third, the schoolmen were wont to express their conception of the Divine Activity in Nature and in Grace by the actual use of the word physical.13 Owen also in his classical work on the Holy Spirit repeatedly affirms the physical nature of the Spirit's operations, especially in the process of regeneration: "There is a real physical work, whereby He infuseth a gracious principle of spiritual life into all that are effectually converted and really regenerated, and without which there is no deliverance from the state of sin and death."

Without agitating the time-honoured questions as to whether this Spiritual Power is mediate or immediate, whether it is resistible or irresistible, whether Spiritual Life is to be considered as part of it, or as the whole, or as none of it; without raising problems suggested by current scientific thought—as to whether there are any analogies between these and the ordinary energies of nature; whether, for instance, they are capable of Transformation, Conservation, or Dissipation—we may rather go on to inquire for the evidence of the spiritual operations themselves and for the results which ought to have followed. It will assist us, however, in understanding the evidence, as well as in defining the kind of result to be looked for, if we take one more backward glance at the two earlier Kingdoms. Suppose we take our stand for a moment on the confines of the Inorganic Kingdom. What order of phenomena will strike us first? Shall we see the Second Kingdom act on the First, and if so, in what particular way?

As we take our first survey of the Inorganic Kingdom we seem to be surrounded by the dead. Every Atom obeys the law of inertia, or yields to simple changes induced by polar, molecular, or other forces. But presently, into this dead world, an unknown Power descends, feels about, seizes certain Atoms, and manipulates them in unprecedented ways. This mysterious Power is the Power of the Kingdom next in order above. To that Kingdom, indeed, the operations of Life, as facts of everyday occurrence, are not mysterious. But to the Atoms they are unintelligible and very wonderful. Here is one Atom raised from the dead. Here is another refusing to bend its will to the attraction of gravity A third, subject to crystalline forces from the beginning, suddenly defies them and takes its place as a part of the higher symmetry of a living organism. As their Fellow-Atoms observe these extraordinary changes, from time to time occurring around them, they have only one word which adequately describes them—they are Miracles.

Taking our stand now on the confines of the Organic, shall we not be presented with the same strange spectacle? Once more we are surrounded by the dead. Once more a Power descends out of another Kingdom—a Kingdom just in order above—and manipulates Organisms in unprecedented ways. Here is one Organism raised from the dead. Here is another refusing to bend its will to the attraction of sin. A third, subject to deforming forces from the beginning, suddenly defies them, and assumes a high and noble spiritual symmetry. And as their Fellow-Organisms observe these changes, their word again is Miracle.

This, then, is what meets us first at the portals of the Third Kingdom—Miracle. We find an order of phenomena strange and inexplicable to the lower Kingdom, but as normal within its own sphere as are the operations of Life in the Organic. As the powers of the Second Kingdom master the First, so the powers of the Third master the Second. But this is not what is usually called Miracle. Miracle is a much narrower thing—so very narrow a thing that up to this point we have scarcely even come in sight of it. To single out a few specific wonders authenticated by ancient documents, and to attach to them the epithet Miracle, is a limitation so monstrous and unwarranted that the protest against it cannot come too soon.

The question of the miraculous is simply the general question of the Third Kingdom. To apply the word to certain acts of healing, to beneficent deeds of an abnormal character, or to deliverance from physical danger, want, or death, is to contemplate the reactions of the Spiritual Kingdom only on the lowest plane of the Organic and Inorganic Worlds. The outstanding miracles, on the contrary, are those effected on the moral and intellectual portions of the highest department of the Organic Kingdom—namely, on the life and character of the Natural Man. The attestation of Christianity is the Christian. Without taking this into account the supernatural changes wrought on the lower department are mere wizard-work. Miracle, from the standpoint of the Second Kingdom, is not alone objectionable as pure prodigy, but it amounts to an absolute breach of Continuity. The sceptical definitions of miracle from this standpoint are perfectly legitimate. Hume is loyal to nature when he affirms that "A miracle is a violation of the laws of nature; and, as a firm and unalterable experience has established these laws, the proof against a miracle, from the very nature of the fact, is as entire as any argument from experience that can possibly be imagined." Deliberately choosing the standpoint of the Second Kingdom, and absolutely rejecting the Third, Hume had no alternative. In his experience of the laws of nature, no variation ever occurred in the usual course of antecedent and consequent. Thus the question of miracle comes to this—there is either delusion, fraud, or a Third Kingdom; and if one rejects the last, his choice between the two former is immaterial.

If, on the other hand, one accepts the Third Kingdom, the miraculous becomes not only credible but necessary The Third Kingdom would not be the Third Kingdom if it could not operate on the Kingdom beneath it in a way which to the Kingdoms below would seem miraculous. The Second

Kingdom is the Second Kingdom because it can operate on the First in a way which to the First must seem miraculous. It is superior to the First in virtue of the superiority of its powers and the corresponding complexity of its organisms. In precisely the same way the Third rises superior to the Second.

It is of much consequence to notice that it is not alone the forms of organisms which are found evolving in nature, but the powers or energies. There is a dynamical as well as a statical evolution. The First Kingdom is equipped with a certain set of powers, or possibly with one central energy capable of assuming varied forms. The Second, while inheriting all this plenishing of the Inorganic Earth, brings upon the scene the new and commanding powers of Life. But the powers of Life, however derived, however directed, are still feeble. The Organic is not always master. And it is not until the Higher Evolution is attained that the complement appears. Then the dominion is complete; that which is perfect is come; and both the First and Second Kingdoms are reigned over by the Third. Were there no domination of the Second by the Third, there had been no Third. And hence the naturalness of our Lord's appeal to miracle as the sign to the Second of the existence of the Third. If a plant wished to convince a mineral of the reality of the powers of the vegetable Kingdom—acting in the direction, let us say, of causing matter to rise in the air during the plant's growth in defiance of gravity—it would naturally point to specific cases where these powers had been exercised. The effect in the first instance upon the mineral would be to tempt it to reject the fact as contrary to experience, but as the evidence accumulated both in quantity and quality the doubt must gradually dissolve. A mineral, subject no longer to the inorganic forces which otherwise reign supreme throughout the Kingdom, bearing practical testimony to the reality and superiority of extra-inorganic powers, would certainly be a phenomenon of transcendent scientific significance. Attention would be gradually drawn to the possibility of the existence of a higher world, and as the facts were seen to be repeated, and as from different quarters evidence accumulated, all doubt upon the subject must gradually dissolve. But if, instead of fixing attention upon an isolated case here and there, one runs his eye over the boundary line dividing the Inorganic from the Organic, and finds the whole frontier abounding in similar activities, like the seaward margin of a coral reef fringed with the living polypes, he receives a new impression of their character and relations. He sees that these marvellous reactions are at that point no longer the exception but the rule. Miracle, in short, is the normal frontier phenomenon. Along the line of junction, again, between the Natural and the Spiritual a similar set of activities are carrying on their ceaseless work. Contemplated from the bottom of the Second Kingdom, where on an isolated group here and there these activities are operating on grosser material, the phenomena are exceptional, unintelligible, and miraculous. But on the frontier they are the normal actions of the Third Kingdom on the Second, demanded by Continuity, justified in the magnitude and gathering potency of their operations by Evolution and susceptible of the same kind of proof.

That they are so little observed in the higher reaches is due to a peculiar law of their being. The Kingdom cometh without observation. But this is not true alone for the Kingdom of God. With infinite gentleness the Second Kingdom throws over the First its mysterious spell. With infinite delicacy its tentacles feel among the all but invisible atoms and build them up into higher forms, by unperceived and silent processes carrying on their growth. All the forces of the Inorganic world even are secret, silent forces. Gravity, the most ponderous of all, came down the ages with a step so noiseless that the world was old before an ear was quick enough to detect its footfall. And the Spiritual forces which carry on the processes to the further stage, re-creating the visible, acting through more and more attenuated forms of matter, become themselves more ethereal, the law in fact being that the various forces decrease in grossness as they increase in power.

But in the first days of Christianity the invisibility of its forces formed a drawback to its development. If not essential, it was at least advisable that the outside world should become at once aware of its pretensions. And if the secret operations of the Spirit in regenerating men were then insufficient to attract attention, it became necessary for the manifestation to descend to what some might call a lower plane. The Spiritual, having power over the whole range of the Organic and Inorganic, might fitly exert an influence in a region where the miracle might be palpable, startling and unmistakable. It might be urged indeed that Virtue could not but go out of Jesus at whatever point He touched life; but at the same time this lower miracle was not due to the inadvertent overflow of a full vessel, but designed to strike men who could not rise to the perception of loftier manifestations. The number of occasions on which He made this concession, always of course with the higher purpose directly in view and apparent in the immediate result, was probably very much larger than the limited information we possess might lead us to suspect. The Evangelists hint that these interpolations of the Higher Powers, these suspensions of the ordinary course of nature in obedience to a higher law, occurred with great frequency. And although it is proper to notice the striking and suggestive fact of the extreme conservation of this power in the life-work of Jesus, it is equally necessary to bear in mind that He continually did works which no other man did, and periodically appealed to these as a ground why the members of the Natural Kingdom should accept the Spiritual.

But there could be no greater mistake than to perpetuate the appeal to this rudimentary form of miracle as the continued attestation of Christianity. If miracle ceased with the first century, our faith, to a large extent, ceases with it, or at least most seriously suffers. What we have to point to now for the credentials of Christianity is not a first series of miracles but the series itself—the series which extends down to the present hour. To ignore this is to put ourselves in a position where belief has everything against it, human testimony notwithstanding. But if we begin with the phenomena which we see around us, or can see if we will, and argue backwards, step by step, coming slowly down to the time when the Miracle Himself was upon the stage, we reach a point where signs and wonders really appear to us as the inevitable. The denial of miracles accordingly, in the ordinary sense, is not the evidence of superior wisdom, but mainly of defective observation. Unless gravity had continued to act during the last two centuries we should, perhaps, have been justified in saying that Newton was mistaken when he saw the apple fall to the ground. How could such a thing happen? Is Newton to contradict "the universal experience of mankind"? Is his testimony to be accepted rather than that of Herschel or Faraday, who never saw such a thing happen? Is not such a violation of the laws of nature altogether incredible and inconceivable, even although the whole of Woolsthorpe were looking over the orchard wall when the apple fell?

Now, if Christianity ceased to act with the first century, I do not see that we can argue for the miraculous. Unless we include the Third Kingdom in our conception a miracle is certainly a violation of the laws of nature. And if the Third Kingdom has passed away miracles may be interesting, but their occupation is gone—there is nothing for them to attest to me. On the other hand, if the Powers of the Third Kingdom are working around me now I am independent of them. I have the superior credential of the "greater works" which Christ's disciples were to do in His name.

But I have said the denial of miracles is due mainly to defective observation—mainly, however, not wholly. The members of the Third Kingdom have something to answer for themselves here. They have failed to provide due materials for observation. Energy may be potential as well as kinetic. Were a visitant from a distant planet who had read "The Correlation of the Physical Forces" or Ganot's "Physics" to land on the coast of Labrador and demand of the Esquimaux to be shown the energies of electricity or the powers of steam, his credulity in his authorities would certainly be shaken. And even if he were informed by a passing Nordenskiold that many of the physical forces were available at Labrador, only the people had never utilized them, his bewilderment would not be lessened. Those who read the Christian's Book hear in like manner of faith to remove mountains, of love stronger than death, of limitless powers to be had for the asking of all the fulness of the Godhead placed at man's disposal. And when they turn to those who know this Book, who profess to believe it, who contribute themselves to the literature of the Third Kingdom, expanding and enforcing its ideas, and almost forcing them on men's attention, what do they see? Is it any satisfaction that a courteous Nordenskiold assures them that these forces are there withal, only the members of this frigid province at the moment do not happen to employ them? For does not the critic see multitudes of individuals met every week for the ostensible purpose of receiving these powers, down on their knees by the thousand crying for them to come? What is he to make of it? Is he dreaming or they? Or does the Kingdom come—but without observation? No; the Kingdom does not come. On the large scale it does not come. The splendid machinery of Christianity is standing still. The Church is paralyzed. When the Second Kingdom asks the Third for its credentials it remains silent. It has something to show in the past; it points sadly to the early centuries. But for the present nothing stirs; it is all as frozen as Labrador.

So men tell us the spiritual energies are a myth—which is as inconclusive as the statement that the physical forces are myths where they are not utilized. The scepticism of the age nevertheless lies at the door of the Church. That there are individuals, and here and there churches, witnessing to the powers of the Third Kingdom is not to be gainsaid. No man who really desires to satisfy himself of the reality of the Spiritual World will seek in vain for a demonstration of the Spirit and of Power. But the appeal is not going forth to all the earth and arresting men by a testimony triumphant and irresistible. The Power that operated at Pentecost is no longer a mighty and awakening force. And even the ethical light which the subjects of the Third Kingdom were admonished to "let shine among men" is all but too dim to see.

Now, whatever may be the state of matters at present within the Visible Church of the Third Kingdom, let us not blind ourselves to the unspeakably important fact that the Spiritual World contains forms of energy infinitely more powerful than those of the First and Second. It has never been sufficiently realized how much greater they are—how much greater they must be, even from analogy. One might almost speak of an Evolution of Energy going on as we rise from higher to higher Kingdoms. By this, of course, is not meant that the higher energy is in any sense evolved from the lower, but that the potency—whatever may be the source of the increment—is found gradually becoming stronger and stronger. As a matter of fact, while the energy within each Kingdom is constant, the organic powers are greater than the inorganic, the Spiritual than either. And the one thing requisite at once for the attestation of the Third Kingdom and the further evolution of the Second is that the subjects of the former should give heed once more to the offer of its King and Founder, "If ye, being evil, know how to give good gifts to your children, much more will your heavenly Father give the Holy Spirit to them that ask it."

The Problem of Foreign Missions

Address delivered at the opening of the session in the Free Church College, Glasgow, in November 1890.

It has for a long time seemed to me that missionary facts, and the missionary problem generally, are susceptible of more special—may I say more scientific?—treatment than they usually receive; and the large size of the field which it has fallen to me to see is favourable to that methodical survey of the whole which is denied even to the missionary, for he represents but a single field.

There are two ways in which men who offer their lives to their fellow-men may regard the world. They mean the same thing in the end, but you will not misunderstand me if I express the apparent distinction in the boldest terms. The first view is that the world is lost and must be saved; the second, that the world is sunken and must be raised. According to the first, the peoples of the world are looked upon as souls—souls to be redeemed; the second thinks of them rather as men—men to be perfected; or as nations—nations to be made righteous. The first deals with a sinner's status in the sight of God, the second with his character in the sight of men The first preaches mainly justification; the second mainly regeneration. The first is the standpoint of the popular evangelism; the second is the view of evolution.

The danger of the first is to save the souls of men and there leave them; the danger of the second is to ignore the soul altogether. As I shall speak now from the last standpoint, I point out its danger at once, and meet it by adding to its watchword, evolution, the qualifying term, Christian. This alone takes account of the whole nature of man, of sin and guilt, of the future and of the past, and recognises the Christian facts and forces as alone adequate to deal with them. The advantage of speaking of "the Christian evolution of the world," instead of, or, at least, as a change from, "the evangelization of the world," will appear as we go on. By making temporary use of the one standpoint, I do not exclude the other; and if I ignore it from this point onward, it is not because it is not legitimate, but simply because it is not the subject.

Nothing ought to be kept more persistently before the mind of those who are open to serve the world as missionaries than the great complexity of the missionary problem; and nothing more strikes one who goes round the world than the amazing variety of work required and the almost radical differences among the various mission fields. In the popular conception the peoples of the world are roughly divided into black and white, or Christian and heathen, and the man who designates himself for the mission field makes a general choice, taking the first opening that comes, and considering but little in his decision that there are many shades of black, and innumerable kinds of heathen. But it is just as absurd for a man to choose in general terms "the foreign field" and go abroad to rescue heathen, as for a planter to go anywhere abroad in the hope of sowing general seed and producing general coffee. The planter soon finds out that there are many soils in the world, some suited to one crop and some to another; that seed must be put in for each particular crop in one way and not in another; that he requires particular implements in each case and not any implements, and that the time between sowing and reaping, and even between sowing and sprouting, is an always appreciable and very varying interval. The mission field has like distinctions. Some crops it is mere waste of time to try to plant in one place; the specialist's business is to find out what will grow there. Some crops will not and cannot come up in one year, or in ten years, or even in fifty years; it is the specialist's business to study scientifically the possibilities of growth, the limitations of growth, and the impossibilities of growth. It is irrational also for the missionary to carry the same message, or rather the same form of message, to every land, or to think that the thought which told to-day will tell tomorrow; he must rotate his crops as God through the centuries rotates the social soil on which they are to grow. To every land he must take, not the general list of agricultural implements furnished by his college, but one or two of special make which possibly his college has never heard of. Above all, when he reaches his field, his duty is to find out what God has grown there already, for there is no field in the world where the Great Husbandman has not sown something. Instead of uprooting his Maker's work and clearing the field of all the plants that found no place in his small European herbarium, he will rather water the growths already there and continue the work at the point where the Spirit of God is already moving. A hasty critic, when these sentences were spoken, construed them into a plea for building up Christianity upon heathenism. The words are "what God has sown there," and "where the Spirit of God is already moving." The missionary problem, in short, so far from being a mere saving of promiscuous souls with a few well-worn appliances, is a most complex question of Social Evolution.

Let me illustrate the necessity of further specialization in regard to missions by reference to the three or four very different fields which I have just visited. As examples of what might be called a scientific classification of missions, one could scarcely pick any more typical than Australia, the South Sea Islands, China, and Japan. I include Australia among mission fields, and I might with it include both British Columbia and Manitoba, because none of these countries can provide as yet for its own evangelization.

I. Australia. The missionary problem, or the mission churches problem, in these colonies is to deal with a civilized people undergoing abnormally rapid development. Australia is a case of prodigiously active growth in a few directions under most favourable natural conditions for nation-making. It is what a biologist would call an organic mass of the highest possible mobility, of almost perilous sensitiveness to prevailing impressions, with feeble safeguards to conserve its solid gains, and few boundary lines either to shape or limit other growths. The orderly progress here is complicated mainly by one thing,—a continuous accretion of outside elements,—due to immigration—which creates difficulties in assimilation. The chief problem of Christianity is to keep pace with the continuous growth; the immediate peril is that it may be wholly ignored in the pressure of competing growths.

II. The South Sea Islands, of which the New Hebrides are a type, lie exactly at the opposite end of the scale. Growth, so far from being active, has not even begun. Here are no nations, scarcely even tribes. The first step in evolution, aggregation, has not yet taken place. These people are still at zero; they are the Amoebae of the human world. There is no complication here of unassimilated elements introduced by immigration, but a serious opposite difficulty—depletion due to emigration to other countries, and to other causes which vitally affect the whole future problem. As to religion here, the field is altogether open, for there is none at all.

III. China. Midway between the South Sea Islands and the Australian colonies, this nation, as every one knows, is an instance of arrested development. On the fair way to become a higher vertebrate, it has stopped short at the crustacean. There are two complications: the amazing strength of the ekoskeleton—the external shell of custom and tradition, so hardened by the deposits of centuries as to make the evolutionist's demand for mobility, i.e. for capacity to change, almost non-existent. Secondly, which directly concerns Christianity, there is a very powerful religion already in possession. These two complications make the missionary problem in China one of the most delicate in the world.

IV. If the South Sea Islands are the opposite of Australia, China, in turn, finds its almost perfect contrast in Japan. One with it in stagnation and isolation from external influences during three thousand years, almost within the last hour Japan has broken what Mr. Bagehot calls its "cake of custom," and so sudden and mature has already been its development that it is, at this moment, demanding from the Powers of Europe political recognition as one of the civilized nations of the world. This is an entirely different case from any of the preceding. It is the insect emerging from the chrysalis. From the Christian standpoint, the case is unique in history. Its own religion was abandoned a few years ago, and the country is at present looking for another.

Even this rough classification will serve to show how far from simple the missionary question really is, how the problem varies from place to place, how different the equipment for each particular field, how wise the mind which should know where to strike in, how responsible the hand which would finger these subtle threads of human destiny, or move among the roots of national life, which God alone has tended in the past. To the

Christian evolutionist these differences are educative. They mark
different stages in the coming of the Kingdom of God on earth, none of
them in vain, all of them to be allowed for, some perhaps to be reset in the
superstructure Christianity would build upon them.

Suppose now the Churches had compiled a classification on some such
lines of all the mission fields of the world, it would serve two practical
purposes. In the first place, it would be the duty of the would-be
missionary to go over that list, and select from it the exact kind of work
to which he was most suited. In this way the missionary staff would be
differentiated with more exactness than at present. Each man, also,
having made his choice, would further equip himself along particular
lines, and become a specialist at his work. In the second place, and what
is just now of even more importance, it would make it possible for some
men to be missionaries, and these among the best men entering the
Universities, who see no room for themselves at present in the foreign
field. Some men with such a review before them might see at once that
there was no place for them in missionary work at all; but others, and, I
believe, a larger number than have ever been attracted by this career,
would find there something open to them—would find in a service which
they had looked upon, perhaps, as somewhat limited and narrow
something which, when looked upon in all its length and breadth, was
large enough and rich enough in practical possibilities to make them offer
to it the whole-hearted work of their lives. To-day, certainly, some of the
best men do go to the foreign field; but the reason why more do not go is
not indifference to its claims, but uncertainty as to whether they are
exactly the type of men wanted, i.e., in plain language, uncertainty as to
whether the cut of their theology quite qualifies them to be the successors
of Carey or Williams. These men feel orthodox enough, of course, to be
clergymen at home, but they have a secret sense that their views might
be scarcely the thing on Eromanga The missionary theology—it is useless
disguising it—is supposed to be a very special article, and a kind of
theological modesty forbids some of our strongest men from considering
it conceivable that they should ever aspire to be missionaries. Now this
feeling is very real, but I am convinced that it is very ignorant—ignorant
of the changed standpoint from which scores of our missionaries are even
now doing their work, ignorant of the world's real needs, ignorant of the
hospitality which they would receive from many at least of the officials of
most of the Mission Boards. And yet these Boards are not wholly guiltless
of having made it appear, or permitting it to continue understood, that
only those of a certain type need look for welcome at their doors. I am not
referring to any particular Church; but I do not think the mission
committees of the world have ever worded an advertisement for men in
language modern enough to include the class of whom I speak. I am not
arguing for free-lances, or budding sceptics, or rationalists being turned
loose on our mission fields. But for young men—and our colleges were
never richer in them than at this moment—who combine with all modern
culture the consecrated spirit and the Christ-like life; for men who are too
honest to go under false pretences to a work which, though they be not yet

specially enthusiastic for it, they are entirely willing to face, there ought to go forth a new and more charitable call. It ought at least to be understood that what qualifies to-day for the leading Churches at home ought not to disqualify for the work of Christ abroad, but that there is for Christian men of the highest originality and power a career in the foreign field at least as great and rational as that at home. Indeed, so far from such men feeling as if they were not wanted in the foreign field, or at the best that their presence there could but be tolerated by the Mission Boards, I am sure the committee at least of some Churches not only want these men to-day, but scarcely want anything else.

First, always, in opening a new mission field comes the splendid work of the pioneer, the old missionary pioneer of the Sunday-school picture books, who stands with his Bible under the stereotyped palm tree, exhorting the crowd of impossible blacks. These we have had in most fields now, and their work must still and always continue. But next we have these same men in settled charges, founding congregations, planting schools, and carrying on the whole evangelical work of the Christian Church. But next, among these, and gathered from these, and in addition to these, we require a further class not wholly absorbed with specific charges, or ecclesiastical progress, or the inculcation of Western creeds, but whose outlook goes forth to the nation as a whole; men who in many ways not directly on the programme of the missionary society will help on its education, its morality, and its healthy progress in all that makes for righteousness. This man, besides being the missionary, is the Christian politician, the apostle of a new social order, the moulder and consolidator of the State. He places the accent, if such an extreme expression of a distinction may be allowed, not on the progress of a Church, but on the coming of the Kingdom of God. He is not the herald, but the prophet of the Cross.

Of course every missionary who nowadays sets out for a foreign field acquires beforehand some general idea of the lie of things in the country to which he goes; but what is needed is more than a general idea. The Christianizing of a nation such as China or Japan is an intricate, ethical, philosophical and social as well as Christian problem; the serious taking of any new country indeed is not to be done by casual sharp-shooters bringing down their man or two here and there, but by a carefully thought out attack upon central points, or by patient siege, planned with all a military tactician's knowledge. We have at present, and, as already said, we shall always need, and they will always do their measure of good, devoted men of the sharp-shooter order who aim at single souls; but in addition to these the Kingdom of God needs men who work with a wider vision—men prepared by fulness of historical, ethnological, and sociological knowledge to become the statesmen of the Kingdom of God.

Let me spend what time remains in briefly expanding the classification already given—partly to illustrate better what I mean, but especially to furnish a few materials to help those whose eyes, when they think of their future life, sometimes turn towards distant lands.

I begin with the New Hebrides—mainly because least is known about them. The New Hebrides mission represents a class of missions differing so essentially from those of the third and fourth classes —China and Japan—that any one who was taught to regard it as a typical mission work would be completely misguided; and for some men at least a mission work of this order would be almost the last thing they would throw themselves into. For what are the real facts? The New Hebrides are a group of small islands, a few about the size of Arran, a very few others two or three times as large, the whole of no geographical importance. They are peopled by beings of the lowest human type to the number of probably not more than 50,000; so that they are of no political importance. This does not refer to the islands, but to the people. The islands themselves are of so great political importance at the present moment that the allegiance of Australia to England would tremble in the balance if there were any suspicion that the Home Government would hand them over to France. The population may be over or under that here stated. I have taken my figures from authorities on the spot, but any approximation to the numbers of inhabitants on these partially explored islands must be a guess. Whether we regard their quality or quantity, they can never play any appreciable part in the world's story; and the question which would immediately rise in the mind of the man who looked at the world from the standpoint of evolution would be the direct one: Is it really worth while sending twenty first-rate men to till this vineyard which can never contribute anything of importance to mankind? If it be replied, But is it proved that they will not? the answer is a sad one. A closer study of these islands shows that instead of increasing their population, these are dying fast. On the first which I visited, Aneityum, when the missionaries reached it, there were some thousands of inhabitants. To-day there is a bare four hundred of depressed and sickly souls. The children are swept away by the white man's epidemics almost as soon as they are born, and the missionaries tell you that the total doom of this island may be a matter of some score years. The very church which was built for the islanders in better days has had to be cut in two, and even the portioned half is now too large; and a small chapel is to be built to hold the remnant of this once noble flock. It is a dismal story, but it is more than likely that it will be repeated in time to a greater or less extent, not only throughout this group, but throughout the whole of the unchristianized South Sea Islands. At New Caledonia I found the depletion of population even more appalling; and though here and there an island may escape, the ultimate prospect is almost total obliteration. This being so, what man who entered the mission field from the standpoint from which I speak, what man who wished his work, however small, to contribute to the permanent evolution of the world, would choose the New Hebrides for his mission field? No man would. Yet is the inference then to be drawn that this mission is a mistake? There is a book by an accomplished clergyman called Wrong Missions to Wrong Races in Wrong Places. Is its thesis, when it answers this question in the affirmative, correct? I should be the last to say so, though its warning is a true one. For, as we have seen, there are missions and missions; and this mission belongs to a type which ought to be more clearly defined and acknowledged.

In the evolutionary branch of missions it has simply no place at all—no place at all. It is a mistake from first to last. But it does not belong to this class, and is not to be judged by its standards—perhaps by higher ones. It belongs to the Order of the Good Samaritan. It is a mission of pure benevolence. Its parallel is the mission of Father Damien on the Leper Island. Who shall say that there are not, and will not always be, men among us who see that kind of mission, men who have no intellectual apprehension of evolution, but who possess the pitiful heart? Or who will say that the day will ever come when the leaders of the wider movement will grudge such men to the lost places of the earth?

I cannot leave this subject without paying my passing tribute—may I say my homage? for tribute they need not—to the missionaries of the New Hebrides themselves. From a recent biography which all of you have read, you know something of the difficulties of their work. You remember the description of the Island of Tanna, the remoteness of its position, the strangeness of its language, the fierceness of its people; you remember how daily the savages sought the missionary's life, and how after years of facing death in a hundred forms he was driven from their shores with scarcely a single convert for his hire. Last June, sailing along Tanna, I tried to land near Mr. Paton's deserted field. With me was one of the missionaries who has now gained a footing on another part of that still cannibal island. As we neared the shore, a hundred painted savages poured from out the woods, and prepared to fire upon us with their guns and poisoned arrows. But the missionary stood up in the bow of the boat and spoke two words to them in their native tongue. Instantly every gun was laid upon the beach, and they rushed into the surf to welcome us ashore. No other unarmed man on this earth could have landed there. It meant that the foundation stone of civilization upon Tanna was already laid. Every island was once like Tanna; some are like it still. But on one after another the cannibal spirit has been already conquered; schools are planted everywhere; and neat churches and manses gleam through the palm trees, and signify to the few ships which wander in those seas that here at least life and property are safe. At Eromanga I went to see the spot on the beach where Williams fell. Hard by were the graves of his murdered successors, Mr. and Mrs. Gordon. Their almost immediate successor, Mr. Robertson, is there to-day, his large church and beautiful manse within a stone-throw of the place where these first martyrs died; his leading elder the son of the cannibal who murdered Gordon. This monster left three sons; they are all elders of the Church, and life is as safe throughout that island to-day as in England. For the first year of their life in Eromanga Mr. and Mrs. Robertson lived in a bullet-proof stockade. They left it only under cover of night for a few yards, and on few occasions, once to bury their firstborn babe. For a year they never saw a European. Their work was to let the people look at them. Their message was to be kind. By-and-by acquaintance was picked up with one or two natives; the circle of influence spread, and after years of extraordinary patience and self-denial, their lives again and again hanging by a thread, they won this island for civilization and Christianity.

On another island, where the missionary two years ago used to see the smoke of the cannibal feasts from his door-step, the natives brought me their spears and bows and poisoned arrows. "We do not need them now," they said; "the missionary has taught us not to kill."

I have no words to express my admiration for these men, and, may I say, their wives, their even more heroic wives; they are perfect missionaries; their toil has paid a hundred times; and I count it one of the privileges of my life to have been one of the few eye-witnesses of their work.

As to the calls of this field for more men, I must add this. It is a proof of the sound sense of the New Hebrides missionaries that they are pretty unanimous in agreeing that, considering the needs of the rest of the world, they have already a quite fair portion of workers. The staff, of course, could be doubled or trebled to-morrow with great advantage, but the missionaries do not ask it. With their present resources and the number of native teachers who are in training they hope in time to cover these islands with mission stations by themselves. I confess these are the least greedy missionaries I ever heard of.

I am sorry that, owing to the shortness of my visit to China, I should feel it a pure presumption to say almost anything about this, the greatest mission field in the world. What I can offer is but a surface impression, and I warn you beforehand it is little worth. From the old standpoint the work in China seems to be splendid; men and women from every Christian Church in the world are busy all over the land, and small congregations of native Christians are springing up everywhere along their track. The industry and devotion of the workers—Roman Catholic, Episcopalian, Congregational, Presbyterian, Wesleyan, and a host of others—is beyond all praise, and there is not one of the missionaries who will not tell you he is encouraged, that he sees some fruit, and that the future is full of hope. There seems to be great care, moreover, in the admission to the Churches of native Christians, and the belief in education and in medical missions is widely rooted. But from the ideal of a Christian evolution there remains very much to criticise—happily less in the direction of commission than of omission. This band of missionaries—I speak not of this society or of that, for the work of each separate society is compact enough in itself, but of the army as a whole—is no steady phalanx set on a fixed campaign, but a disordered host of guerillas recruited from all denominations, wearing all uniforms, and waging a random fight. Some are equipped with obsolete weapons, some with modern armament; but they possess no common programme or consistent method. Besides being confusing to the Chinese, this means great waste of power, great loss of cumulative effect. This, of course, is inevitable at first, and it is not the sin of the missionaries, but of Christendom; and, after the late Shanghai conference, there is more than a hope that even this in time may be remedied. But what one would really like to see, in addition to greater concentration, would be a more serious reconsideration of the manner of approach and the form of message most suited to the Chinese mind, and nature, and tradition, and some further contribution to the question how far its form of Christianity is to be Western, or how far a Chinese basis is possible or permissible. These questions might be left to adjust themselves but for one most serious fact: the converts in China, in the majority of districts, are almost exclusively drawn at present from the lower classes. There are exceptions, but the educated classes as a whole, the merchants and the mandarins, remain, I understand, almost wholly untouched. There is something wrong if this be the case. And leaving the present machinery to do the good work it is doing among the poor, I would join with the best of the missionaries in arguing for a few Rabbis to be sent to China, or to be picked from our fine scholars already there, who would quietly reconnoitre the whole situation, and shape the teaching of the country along well-considered lines—men, especially, who would lay themselves out through education, lectures, preaching, and literature to reach the intellect of the Empire. That some men are aiming at this, and doing it splendidly, we are already well aware. It is the direct policy of many missionaries and even of whole societies. But it is these missionaries themselves who are crying out for more of it. Men will not take the trouble to enquire what some of these societies are really aiming at and really doing, and, in ignorance of either, they regard the whole missionary work as a waste of time and money. The things also which one hears of missionaries, in talking with the business men of the Eastern ports—the contempt, the charges of inefficiency, impracticableness, and general uselessness—are enough to make any traveller not well on his guard renounce the mission cause for ever. These impressions are reimported into this country by ninety out of every hundred men who return home from the great commercial houses of the East, and they build up a public opinion against foreign missions most wanton and most false. As a rule these critics have never had ten minutes' serious talk with a missionary in their lives. If they had, they would find two things. First, that there were some missionaries a thousand times worse in folly and incompetence than they had ever imagined; and, secondly, that there were others, and these by far the greater majority, than whom no wiser, saner, more practical men could be found in any of the business houses of the world. It is men of this latter class, and not merely the passing traveller, who are calling out to-day for more scientific work and more rational methods in the mission field. They are perfectly aware that the evangelization of China is not a mere carrying of the Gospel to illiterate and heathen savages; and that perfect knowledge both of the modes of thought of the people and of the true genius of Christianity is needed to direct a campaign that will be permanently effective there. The missionary who is an educationist, who has some scientific and philosophic training, who knows something of sociology and political economy, and who will apply these in Christian forms to China, is the man most needed there at the present hour. For it is to be remembered that this is a case of arrested motion, and that the most natural development, perhaps the only possible one, certainly the only permanent one, will be one which is a continuation of that already begun rather than one entirely abnormal and foreign.

It was new to me, though I ought to have known it before, that the Chinese, instead of looking up to Europeans, regard them as a most inferior and even barbaric people—clever, certainly, in a few directions, but with no sort of authority to instruct a Celestial. In most mission fields the missionary has a platform simply in the fact that he is a white man, that he came in a steam ship, and wears a hat; but the Chinaman has no such hallucination. He listens to a European missionary much as a London crowd would listen to a Red Indian—half curious, half amused, but wholly contemptuous as to his pretension to teach him anything. It is the deliberate opinion of many men who know China intimately, who are sympathetic with missionaries, who are even missionaries themselves, that half of the preaching, and especially the itinerating preaching, now being carried on throughout the Empire is absolutely useless. Some go so far as to say that it even does harm, that its ignorance and general quality make it almost an impertinence. In New York I met an influential Christian layman, who had just returned from a visit to China, where his son was a missionary; and he assured me that he meant to devote this entire winter to opening the eyes of the American Churches to the futility and falseness of method of much that was being done being done in perfect good faith—by worthy men and worthy women to convert the people of China. I cannot verify this criticism; I merely record it. But at a time when the loud cry for hundreds of more laymen to pour into China is sounding over this land the warning ought at least to be heard. I go further. This call is frequently uttered in such terms as to take almost an unfair advantage of a certain class of Christians—uttered with a harrowing importunity and sensationalism of appeal which when it falls upon a tender conscience or an excited mind makes it seem blasphemy to decline. The kind of missionary secured by this process, to say the least, is neither the wisest nor the best; and not only China needs to be protected from these men, but they need to be protected from themselves and from those who, in genuine but unbalanced zeal, appeal to them—protected by sober statements from sober men, who love the word of God, and the souls of men not less, but who understand both better.

I pass now to a country where the situation is more delicate still. Japan is the most interesting country in the world at this moment. The past never witnessed a birth of a civilized nation so remarkable, so orderly, so sudden. Within the lifetime of all of us the Japanese were a wholly unilluminated race. They kept their doors shut against outside influence of every kind. No foreigner could even enter the land. Today all is changed. They sent envoys to France, who brought back law; others to Germany, who gave them a military organization. From England they borrowed a navy; from America a system of national education. From the civilized world in general they imported a most perfect telegraph and postal system, railways and tramways, the electric light, Universities, technical colleges, and within the last few months, Houses of Parliament and a vote. The Japanese have set themselves up, in short, with all the material and machinery of an advanced and rising civilized State—all the material except one. They have no religion. As was inevitable, heathenism has been abolished, and, as already said, the people are in the unique position at present of prospecting for a religion.

Now this last fact having become somewhat known, Japan to-day presents the spectacle of having already within its borders representatives from every Church in Christendom prospecting for converts. Even the politicians being fairly agreed—and this in itself is most striking—that some sort of religion is necessary, these representatives are eagerly listened to, and get a perfectly honest chance.

The noblest building in the capital of Japan is the Cathedral of the Greek Church. Roman Catholics are there, Unitarians are there, Episcopalians of different degrees of height and Presbyterians of different degrees of breadth, and Methodists of different degrees of heat, and Baptists and Independents, and Theosophists and Spiritualists, and every sect and church and denomination under heaven. The issue will be one of the most interesting events in ecclesiastical history. For there is no favouritism and no prejudice. When the result is known, it will be the purest possible case of the survival of the fittest.

One cannot at all say at present who has it. It will be some sort of Christianity; probably not now the Roman Catholic or the Greek; and what makes the situation so extremely interesting and the hour so overwhelmingly important is that every Christian man, and every Christian book, and every Christian stroke of work that are given to Japan have an immediate and almost palpable influence upon this problem. Such is the mood and such is the malleability of this nation at the present hour, that if a Christian of great size arose to-morrow, either among the Japanese themselves or among the European missionaries, he could almost give the country its religion. If there be here one prophet, or half a prophet, or even the making of half a prophet, let me assure him that there is no field in the world to-day where, so far as man can judge, his best years could be lived to so great a purpose.

With the mention of two more facts, I am done with Japan. You are aware that the work of the missionaries has been so successful that there are already thousands upon thousands of Christian converts in the country. Very many of these know English as well as we do, and many are perfectly read in every form of modern European literature, and as able and as cultured as the picked men in our Universities. The man among these men whom I found was most regarded as a leader of thought among the Japanese Christians made to me this striking statement: "We have got," he said, "our Christianity almost exclusively from the missionaries, especially from the American missionaries, and we can never thank them enough. But after a little we began to look at it for ourselves, and we made a discovery. We found that Christianity was a greater and a richer thing than the missionaries told us. Perhaps they themselves were second-handed. At any rate, we must henceforth look at it for ourselves. We want Christianity, not perhaps necessarily a Western Christianity."

His next sentence was expressed with some hesitation and much delicacy, but it meant this—"In the past they have helped us much; but . . . they may now . . . go."

In justice to the missionaries, let me say that one or two of the few whom I met were quite aware that this feeling existed towards some of them, and they also knew its cause; others knew that the Japanese were beginning to think them de trop, but they attributed it to conceit, and to the general anti-English reaction lately set in in all departments But all were agreed that the Japanese church could not yet be left to stand alone. What exactly my critic would have replied, or rather how exactly he would have qualified by further statement of his meaning, may possibly be inferred from the other circumstances which I wish to name. It happened in Tokio that I had the privilege of addressing some thirty or forty Japanese Christian pastors. At the close I asked them if they had any message they would like me to take home with me to the Churches here or in America. They appointed a spokesman, who stood up and told me, in their name, that there were two things they would like me to say. The one was, "Tell them to send us one six thousand dollar missionary, rather than ten two thousand dollar missionaries." But the second request went deeper. I again give the exact words—"Tell them," he said, "that we want them to send us no more doctrines. Japan wants Christ."

I trust the narrative of these two facts will not be taken as a reproach to the missionaries. If they represent a true feeling, it is rather to their lasting honour that in a few years they should have taught the native Christians to see so far. Of the actual mission work in Japan I can say nothing, for I was only a few days there. But if I were to judge from the Japanese converts whom I met, I would question whether any mission work in the world had ever produced fruit of so fine a quality. How deep it is, how permanent it is, remain for the test of time to declare; but the immediate outlook, though disheartening possibly to individual missionaries, seems to me one of the richest hope and promise.

I had meant in closing to turn to Australia and make a bid for able men for that Greater Britain, but there is only time for a word. Composed largely of men whom the rush for wealth has drawn from an older civilization, the Church's problem in that colossal continent—you are aware it is as big as Europe—is to establish the new civilization in truth and righteousness. Who, where every man is making money, is to make just laws, to raise social standards, to purify political ideals? Two kinds of ministers are required to be directly or indirectly the leaders of this work.

(1) Men of the highest culture and ability as ministers for the large towns; men who are preachers and students. There is no more influential sphere in the world than that open to a cultured preacher in one of the capital cities of Australia. His influence will tell upon the whole colony almost immediately, and as a public man he will have opportunities of giving a tone and direction even to political life such as no one at home possesses. At this moment there are some three or four vacant churches of the very first rank which must be supplied from home; and if these are

shut to students or probationers, any man of strength in that new land can raise a minor charge to an equal place within two or three years' time.

(2) The second kind of man that is wanted, and he is wanted not by the dozen, but by the score, is the bush minister. This man must be a man; he must be ready, and adaptable; he may be as unprofessional as he pleases, but he must be a Christian gentleman. His work will be to keep up an occasional service at some half-dozen wooden chapels—oases in the wilderness of forest and scrub—or to hold services in barns or, on great occasions, in some village church. You will see why I have allocated the man who is the student to the city. This man cannot study, or cannot study much. He is the evangelist, the other the teacher.

* * * * *

If one saw a single navvy trying to remove a mountain, the desolation of the situation would be appalling. Most of us have seen a man, or two, or a hundred or two—ministers, missionaries, Christian laymen—at work upon the higher evolution of the world; but it is when one sees them by the thousand in every land, and in every tongue, and the mountain honey-combed and slowly crumbling on each of its frowning sides, that the majesty of the missionary work fills and inspires the mind.

* * * * *

Gentlemen, finally, what a field the world is for any man who means, as Goethe says, to be a hammer and not an anvil! We have looked down only three or four of the vistas of useful work which in every region of the earth are opening up; but how attractive, how alluring each of them is to the man with a generous purpose in his soul! There is one thing for which I love the very sound of the word Evolution—its immense hope, its indescribable faith. Darwin's great discovery, or the discovery which he brought into prominence, is the same as Galileo's—that the world moves. The Italian prophet said it moved from West to East, the English philosopher said it moved from low to high. The message of science to this age is that all Nature is on the side of the men or of the nation who is trying to rise. An ascending energy is in the universe, and the whole moves on with the mighty idea and anticipation of the Ascent of Man.

The progress of the past seems almost to guarantee the future. Here there may be retardation, there obstruction, but somehow we have learned to believe that the mass moves on. Yesterday saw divergence from the faith, to-day mourned persecution; but somehow to-morrow we feel that the sun will shine again on a Kingdom of God which has also somehow grown. After all, this instrument of science, this discoverer of a secret motion in the world, this great calmer of faithless men, this rebuker of quaking saints, is a religious teacher—we work with it, we look with its eyes, we hear its voice, and it says with Browning—

"God's in His Heaven,
All's right with the world."

The Contribution of Science to Christianity

There is nothing more inspiring just now to the religious mind than the expansion of the intellectual area of Christianity. Christianity seemed for a time to have ceased to adapt itself to the widening range of secular knowledge, and the thinking world had almost left its side. But the expansion of Christianity can never be altogether contemporaneous with the growth of knowledge. For new truth must be solidified by time before it can be built into the eternal truth of the Christian system. Yet, sooner or later, the conquest comes; sooner or later, whether it be art or music, history or philosophy, Christianity utilises the best that the world finds, and gives it a niche in the temple of God.

To the student of God's ways, who reverently marks His progressive revelation and scans the horizon for each new fulfilment, the field of science presents just now a spectacle of bewildering interest. To say that he regards it with expectation is feebly to realize the dignity and import of the time. He looks at science with awe. It is the thing that is moving, unfolding. It is the breaking of a fresh seal. It is the new chapter of the world's history. What it contains for Christianity, or against it, he knows not. What it will do, or undo—for in the fulfilling it may undo—he cannot tell. The plot is just at its thickest as he opens the page; the problems are more in number and more intricate than they have ever been before, and he waits almost with excitement for the next development.

And yet this attitude of Christianity towards science is as free from false hope as it is from false fear. It has no false fear, for it knows the strange fact that this plot is always at its thickest; and its hope of a quick solution is without extravagance, for it has learned the slowness of God's unfolding and His patient tempering of revelation to the young world which has to bear the strain. But, for all this, we cannot open this new and closely written page as if it had little to give us. With nature as God's work; with man, God's finest instrument, as its investigator; with a multitude of the finest of these finest instruments, in laboratory, field, and study, hourly engaged upon this book, exploring, deciphering, sifting, and verifying—it is impossible that there should not be a solid, original, and ever-increasing gain. Add to this man's known wish to know more, and God's wish that he should know more—for nature is fuller of nothing than of invitations to learn—and we shall see how true it is that nature has but to be asked, to give her best.

The one thing to be careful about in approaching nature is, that we really come to be taught; and the same attitude is honourably due to its interpreter, science. Religion is probably only learning for the first time how to approach science. Their former intercourse, from faults on both sides, and these mainly due to juvenility, is not a thing to remember. After the first quarrel—for they began the centuries hand in hand—the question of religion to science was simply, "How dare you speak at all?" Then as science held to its right to speak just a little, the question became, "What new menace to our creed does your latest discovery portend?" By-and-by both became wiser, and the coarser conflict ceased. Then we find religion suggesting a compromise, and asking simply what particular adjustment to its last hypothesis science would demand. But we do not speak now of the right to be heard, or of menaces to our faith, or even of compromises. Our question is a much maturer one—we ask what contribution science has to bestow, what good gift the wise men are bringing now to lay at the feet of our Christ. This question marks an immense advance in the relation between science and Christianity, and we should be careful to sustain it. Nothing is more easily thrown out of working order than the balance between different spheres of thought. The least assumption of superiority on the part of one, the least hint of a challenge, even a suggestion of independence, may provoke a quarrel. In one sense religion is independent of science, but in another it is not. For science is not independent of religion, and religion dare not leave it. One notices sometimes a disposition in religious writers, not only to make light of the claims of science, to smile at its attempts to help them, to despise its patronage, but even to taunt it with its impotence to touch the higher problems of life and being at all. Now science has feelings. This impotence is a fact, but it is the limitation simply of its function in the scheme of thought; and to taunt it with its insufficiency to perform other functions is a vulgar way to make it jealous of that which does perform them. We live in an intellectual commune, and owe too much to each other to reflect on a neighbour's poverty, even when it puts on appearances.

The result of the modern systematic study of nature has been to raise up in our midst a body of truth with almost unique claims to acceptance. The grounds of this acceptance are laid bare to all the world. There is nothing esoteric about science. It has no secrets. Its facts can be seen and handled: they are facts; they are nature itself. Apart therefore from their attractiveness or utility, men feel that here at last they have something to believe in, something independent of opinion, prejudice, self-interest, or tradition. This feeling is a splendid testimony to man as well as to nature. And we do not grudge to science the vigour and devotion of its students, for, like all true devotion, it is founded on an intense faith. Now the mere presence of this body of truth, so solid, so transparent, so verifiable, immediately affects all else that lies in the field of knowledge. And it affects it in different ways. Some things it scatters to the winds at once. They have been the birthright of mankind for ages, it may be; their venerableness matters not, they must go. And the power of the new-comer is so self-evident that they require no telling, but disappear of themselves. In this way the modern world has been rid of a hundred superstitions.

Among other things which have been brought to this bar is Christianity. It knows it can approve itself to science; but it is taken by surprise, and therefore begs time. It will honestly look up its credentials and adjust itself, if necessary, to the new relation. Now this is the position of theology at the present moment. The purification of religion, Herbert Spencer tells us, has always come from science. In this case it is largely true. And theology proceeds by asking science what it demands, and then borrows its instruments to carry out the improvements. This loan of the instruments constitutes the first great contribution of science to religion.

What are these instruments? We shall name two—the Scientific Method and the Doctrine of Evolution. The first is the instrument for the interpretation of Nature; the second is given us as the method of Nature itself. With the first of these we shall deal formally; the second will present itself in various shapes as we proceed.

In emphasizing the scientific method as a contribution from science to Christianity, it is not to be understood that science has an exclusive, or even a prior claim, either to its discovery or possession. Along with the germs of all great things, it is found in the Bible; and theologians all along have fallen into its vein at times, though they have seldom pursued it long or with entire abandonment. There are examples of work done in modern theology, German and English, by the use of this method, which for the purity, consistency, and reverence with which it is applied are not surpassed by anything that physical science has produced. At the same time, this is par excellence the method of science. The perfecting of the instrument, the most lucid exhibition of its powers, the education in its use, above all the intellectual revolution which has compelled its application in every field of knowledge, we owe to natural science. Theology has had its share in this great movement, how much we need not ask, or seek to prove. The day is past for quarrelling over rights of discovery; and whether we owe the scientific method to Job and Paul, or to Bacon and Darwin, is just the kind of question which the possession of this instrument would warn us not to touch.

To see what the scientific method has done for Christianity, we have only to ask ourselves what it is. The things which it insists upon are mainly two—the value of facts, and the value of laws. From the first of these comes the integrity of science; from the second its beauty and force. On bare facts science from first to last is based. Bacon's contribution to science was simply that he vindicated the place and power, the eternal worth, of facts; Darwin's, that he supplied it with facts. Now if Christianity possesses anything it possesses facts. So long as the facts were presented to the world Christianity spread with marvellous rapidity. But there came a time when the facts were less exhibited to men than the evidence for the facts. Theology, that is to say, began to rest on authority. Men or manuscripts were quoted as authorities for these facts, always with a loss of impressiveness, a loss increasing rapidly as time distanced the facts themselves. Then as the facts became more and more remote the

Churches became the authorities rather than individual witnesses, and this was accompanied by a still further loss of power. And the surest proof of the waning influence of the facts themselves, and the extent of the loss incurred by the transfer of their credential to authority, is found in the appeal, which quickly followed, to the secular arm. The facts, ceasing to be their own warrant, had to be enforced by the establishment of judicial relations between Church and State. It is these intermediaries between the facts and the modern observer that stumble science. Its method is not to deal with persons however exalted, nor with creeds however admirable, nor with Churches however venerable. It will look at facts and at facts alone. The dangers, the weakness, the unpracticableness in some cases of this method, are well known. Nevertheless it is a right method. It is the method of all reformation; it was the method of the Reformation. The Reformation was largely a revolt against intermediaries, an appeal to facts. Now Christianity is learning from science to go back to its facts, and it is going back to facts. Critics in every tongue are engaged upon the facts; travellers in every land are unveiling facts; exegetes are at work upon the words, scholars upon the manuscripts; sceptics, believing and unbelieving, are eliminating the not-facts; and the whole field is alive with workers. And the point to mark is that these men are not manipulating, but verifying, facts.

There is one portion of this field of facts, however, which is still strangely neglected, and to which a scientific theology may turn its next attention. The evidence for Christianity is not the Evidences. The evidence for Christianity is a Christian. The unit of physics is the atom, of biology the cell, of philosophy the man, of theology the Christian. The natural man, his regeneration by the Holy Spirit, the spiritual man and his relations to the world and to God, these are the modern facts for a scientific theology. We may indeed talk with science on its own terms about the creation of the world, and the spirituality of nature, and the force behind nature, and the unseen universe; but our language is not less scientific, not less justified by fact, when we speak of the work of the risen Christ, and the contemporary activities of the Holy Ghost, and the facts of regeneration, and the powers which are freeing men from sin. There is a great experiment which is repeated every day, the evidence for which is as accessible as for any fact of science; its phenomena are as palpable as any in nature; its processes are as explicable, or as inexplicable; its purpose is as clear; and yet science has never been seriously asked to reckon with it, nor has theology ever granted it the place its impressive reality commands. One aim of a scientific theology will be to study conversion, and restore to Christianity its most powerful witness. When men, by mere absorption in the present, refuse to consider history, or from traditional prejudice take refuge in the untrustworthiness of the records, it is unwise to refer, in the first place at least, to phenomena which are centuries old, when we have the same among us now.

But not less essential, in the scientific method, than the examination of facts is the arrangement of them under laws. And the work of modern science in this direction has resulted in its grandest achievement—the demonstration of the uniformity of nature. This doctrine must have an immediate effect upon the entire system of theology. For one thing, the contribution of the spiritual world to the uniformity of nature has yet to be made. Not that the natural world is to include the spiritual, but that a higher natural will be seen to include both. It cannot be said that Christianity as arranged by theology at present is highly natural, nor can it be said to be unnatural. In that relation it is simply neutral. The question of naturalness or the reverse is one which has not hitherto at all concerned it. There was no call upon theology to make its presentation of itself with a view to nature, and therefore, if that is an advisable thing, or a feasible thing, it has yet, on the large scale at least, to be attempted. In the natural world, the truth of the uniformity of nature took a long time to grow. No one in the first instance set himself to establish it. Innumerable workers in innumerable fields, engaged upon different classes of facts, found a mysterious brotherhood of common laws. Again and again, and everywhere again and again, the same familiar lines confronted them, few, simple, and unchangeable, yet each with a vanishing trend towards an upward point, hidden as yet in mystery. These workers did not formally consult together about these laws, or seek to follow them beyond the line of sight. Nor did they try to find a name for the hidden point to which all converged. But there grew up amongst them a sense of symmetry in the whole which found expression in the formula, which is now the postulate of science—the "uniformity of nature." In the same way probably shall we one day see disclosed the uniformity of the spiritual world. The earlier work had to be accomplished first, the scaffolding for the inner temple; but when the whole is finished there will be nothing in the spiritual world to put the mind of science to confusion. The laws of both as they radiate upwards will meet in a common cupola, and between the outer and the inner courts the priests of nature and the priests of God will go in and out together.

There may be laws, or actings, in the spiritual world, which it may seem to some impossible to include in such a scheme. God is not, in theology, a Creator merely, but a Father; and according to the counsel of His own will He may act in different cases in different ways. To which the reply is that this also is law. It is the law of the Father, the law of the paternal relation, the law of the free-will; yet not an exceptional law, it is the law of all fathers of all free-wills. Besides, if in the private Christian life the child of God finds dealings which are not reducible to law, grant even their lawlessness if that be possible, that is a family matter, a relation of parent and child, similar to the earthly relation, and scarcely the kind of case to be referred to science. Into ordinary family relations science rarely feels called to intrude; and it is obvious that in dealing with this class of cases in the spiritual world, science is attempting a thing which in the natural world it leaves alone. If ethics chooses to take up these questions, it has more right to do so; but that there should be a reserve in the spiritual world for God acting towards His children in a way past finding out is what would be expected from the mere analogies of the family. It is a pity this distinction between the paternal and the governmental relation of God is not more apprehended by science; for there is an indelicacy about all these questions which arises from ignorance of it—questions concerning prayer and natural law, "special providences," and others—which is painful to devout people. It is not by any means that religion cannot afford to have these things talked of, but they are to be approached in privacy, with the sympathy and respect due to family affairs.

The relations of the spiritual man, however, are not all, or nearly all, in this department. There are whole classes of facts in the outer provinces which have yet to be examined and arranged under appropriate laws. The intellectual gain to Christianity of such a process will be obvious. But there is also a practical gain to the religious experience of not less moment. Science is nothing if not practical, and the scientific method has little for Christianity after all if it is not to exalt and enrich the lives of its followers. It is worth while, therefore, taking a single example of its practical value.

The sense of lawlessness which pervades the spiritual world at present re-acts in many subtle and injurious ways upon the personal experience of Christians. They gather the idea that things are managed differently there from anywhere else—less strictly, less consistently; that blessings or punishments are dispensed arbitrarily, and that everything is ordered rather by a Divine discretion than by a system of fixed principle. In this higher atmosphere ordinary sequences are not to be looked for—cause and effect are suspended or superseded. Accordingly, to descend to the particular, men pray for things which they are quite unable to receive, or altogether unwilling to pay the price for. They expect effects without touching the preliminary causes, and causes without calculating the tremendous nature of the effects. There is nothing more appalling than the wholesale way in which unthinking people plead to the Almighty the richest and most spiritual of His promises, and claim their immediate fulfilment, without themselves fulfilling one of the conditions either on which they are promised or can possibly be given. If the Bible is closely looked into, it will probably be found that very many of the promises have attached to them a condition—itself not unfrequently the best part of the promise. True prayer for any promise is to plead for power to fulfil the condition on which it is offered, and which, being fulfilled, is in that act given. We have need, certainly in this sense, to know more of prayer and natural law. And science could make no truer contribution to modern Christianity than to enforce upon us all, as unweariedly as in nature, the law of causation in the spiritual life. The reason why so many people get nothing from prayer is that they expect effects without causes; and this also is the reason why they give it up. It is not irreligion that makes men give up prayer, but the uselessness of their prayers.

There is one other gain to Christianity to be expected from the wider use of the scientific method which may be mentioned in passing. Besides transforming it outwardly and reforming it inwardly, it must attract an ever-increasing band of workers to theology. There is a charm in working with a true method, which, once felt, becomes for ever irresistible. The activity in theology at the present time is almost limited, and the enthusiasm almost wholly limited, to those who are working with the scientific method. Round the islands of coral skeletons in the Pacific Ocean there is a belt of living coral. Each tiny polyp on this outermost fringe, and here only, secretes a solid substance from the invisible storehouse of the sea, and lays down its life in adding it to the advancing reef. So science and so theology grow. Through these workers on the fringing reef—behind, in contact with the great solid, essential, formulated past; before, the profound sea of unknown truth—through these workers, and through these alone, can knowledge grow. The phalanx of able, busy, and joyful spirits crowding the growing belt of each modern science—electricity, for example —may well excite the envy of theology. And it is the method that attracts them. And every day theology too, as it knows this method, gets busier—not undermining the old reef, nor abandoning it to make a new one, but adding the living work of living men to this essential, formulated past.

We are warned sometimes that this method has dangers, and told not to carry it too far. It is then it becomes dangerous. The danger arises, not from the use of the scientific method, but from its use apart from the scientific spirit. For these two are not quite the same. Some men use the scientific method, but not in the scientific spirit. And as science can help Christianity with the former, Christianity may perhaps do something for science as regards the latter. Christianity is certainly wonderfully tolerant of all this upturning in theology, wonderfully generous and patient and hopeful upon the whole. And so just is the remark of "Natural Religion," that the true scientific spirit and the Christian spirit are one, that the Christian world is probably prepared to accept almost anything the most advanced theology brings, provided it be a joint product of the scientific spirit—the fearlessness and originality of the one, tempered by the modesty, caution, and reverence of the other.

To preserve this confidence, and to keep this spirit pure, is a sacred duty. There is an intellectual covetousness abroad just now which is neither the fruit nor the friend of a scientific age—a haste to be wise, which, like the haste to be rich, leads men into speculation upon indifferent securities, and can only end in fallen fortunes. Theology must not be bound up with such speculation. "If"—to recall one of the fine outbursts of Bacon—"if there be any humility towards the Creator, any reverence for or disposition to magnify His works, any charity for man and anxiety to relieve his sorrows and necessities, any love of truth in nature, any hatred of darkness, any desire for the purification of the understanding, we must entreat men again and again to discard, or at least set apart for the while, these volatile and preposterous philosophies which have preferred these to hypotheses, led experience captive, and triumphed over the works of God; and to approach with humility and veneration to unroll the volume of creation, to linger and meditate therein, and with minds washed clean from opinions to study it in purity and integrity. For this is that sound and language which 'went forth into all lands' and did not incur the confusion of Babel; this should men study to be perfect in, and becoming again as little children, condescend to take the alphabet of it into their hands, and spare no pains to search and unravel the interpretation thereof, but pursue it strenuously and persevere even unto death." The one safeguard is to use the intellectual method in sympathetic association with the moral spirit. The scientific method may bring to light many fresh and revolutionary ideas; the scientific spirit will see that they are not given a place as dogmas in their first exuberance, that they are held with caution, and abandoned with generosity on sufficient evidence. The scientific method may secure many new and unique possessions; the scientific spirit will wear its honours humbly, knowing that after all new truth is less the product of genius than the daughter of time. And in its splendid progress the scientific method will find some old lights dim, some cherished doctrines old-fashioned, venerable authorities superseded; the scientific spirit will be respectful to the past, checking that mockery at the old which those who lack it make unthinkingly, and remembering that the day will come for its work also to pass away.

So much for the scientific method. Let us now consider for a moment one or two of its achievements. Apart from the usual reservations, which it is hoped are always implied—that science is only in its infancy, that the scientific method is almost still a novelty, that therefore we are not to expect too much nor to be absolutely sure of what we get—there is a special reason in this case for remembering that science is new. For this will prepare us to expect its contribution to theology—its contribution, that is, where the actual subject-matter of laws and discoveries of science are involved, its method—in one direction rather than in another, and in certain departments rather than others. Itself at an elementary stage, we should be wrong to look for any very pronounced contribution as yet to the higher truths of religion We should expect the first effect among the elements of religion. We should expect science to be fairly decided in its utterances about them, to become more and more hesitating as it runs up the range of Christian doctrine, and gradually to lapse into silence. Proceeding upon this principle we should go back at once to Genesis. We should begin with the beginnings, and expect the first serious contribution to theology on the doctrine of creation.

And what do we find? We find that upon this subject of all others science has most to offer us. It comes to us freighted with vast treasures of newly noticed facts, but with a theory which by many thoughtful minds has been accepted as the method of creation. And, more than this, it tells us candidly it has failed—and the failures of science are among its richest contributions to Christianity—it has failed to discover any clue to the ultimate mystery of origins, any clue which can compete for a moment with the view of theology.

Consider first this impressive silence of science on the question of origins. Who creates, or evolves? whether do the atoms come, or go? These questions remain as before. Science has not found a substitute for God. And yet, in another sense, these questions are very different from before. Science has put them through its crucible. It took them from theology, and deliberately proclaimed that it would try to answer them. They are now handed back, tried, unanswered, but with a new place in theology and a new power with science. Science has attained, after this ordeal, to a new respect for theology. If there are answers to these questions, and there ought to be, theology holds them And theology likewise has learned a new respect for science. In its investigations of these questions science has made a discovery. It has seen plainly that atheism is unscientific. It is a remarkable thing that after trailing its black length for centuries across European thought, atheism should have had its doom pronounced by science. With its most penetrating gaze science has now looked at the back of phenomena. It says: "The atheist tells us there is nothing there. We cannot believe him. We cannot tell what it is, but there is certainly something. Agnostics we may be, we can no longer be atheists."

This permission to theism to go on, this invitation to Christianity to bring forward its theory to supplement science here, and give this something a name, is a great advance. And science has not left here a mere vague void for Christianity to fill, but a carefully defined niche with suggestions of the most striking kind as to how it is to be filled. It has never been sufficiently noticed how complete is the scientific account of a creative process, and how here biology and theology have actually touched. Watch a careful worker in science for a moment, and see how nearly a man by searching has found out God. The observer is Mr. Huxley. He stands looking down the tube of a powerful microscope. Almost touching the lens, he has placed a tiny speck of matter, which he tells us is the egg of a little water-animal, the common salamander or water-newt. He is trying to describe what he sees; it is the creation or development of a life. "It is a minute spheroid," he says, "in which the best microscope will reveal nothing but a structureless sac, enclosing a glairy fluid, holding granules in suspension. But strange possibilities lie dormant in that semi-fluid globe. Let a moderate supply of warmth reach its watery cradle, and the plastic matter undergoes changes so rapid and yet so steady and purposelike in their succession, that one can only compare them to those operated by a skilled modeller upon a formless lump of clay. As with an invisible trowel the mass is divided and sub-divided into smaller and smaller portions, until it is reduced to an aggregation of granules not too large to build withal the finest fabrics of the nascent organism. And then it is as if a delicate finger traced out the line to be occupied by the spinal column, and moulded the contour of the body; pinching up the head at one end, and the tail at the other, and fashioning flank and limb into due salamandrine proportions in so artistic a way, that, after watching the process hour by hour, one is almost involuntarily possessed by the notion that some more subtle aid to vision than an achromatic would show the hidden artist with his plan before him, striving with skilful manipulation to perfect his work."[15] So near has this observer come to a creator from the purely scientific side, that he can only describe what he sees in terms of creation. From the natural side he has come within a hair's-breadth of the spiritual. Science and theology are here simply touching each other. There is not room really for another link between. And it will be apparent, on a moment's reflection, that we have much more in this than the final completion of a religious doctrine. What we really have is the joining of the natural and spiritual worlds themselves. It seems such a long way, to some men, from the natural to the spiritual, that it is a relief to witness at last their actual contact even at a point. And this is also a presumption that they are in unseen contact all along the line; that as we push all other truths to the last resort they will be met at the point where they disappear, that the complementary relations of religion and science will more and more be manifest; and that the unity, though never the fusion of the natural and the spiritual will be finally disclosed.

When we turn now to the larger question of the creation of the world itself, we find much more than silence, or a permission to go on. We find science has a definite theory on that subject. It offers, in short, to theology, a doctrine of the method of creation, in its hypothesis of evolution. That this doctrine is proved yet, no one will assert. That in some of its forms it is never likely to be proved, many are convinced. It will be time for theology to be unanimous about it when science is unanimous about it. Yet it would be idle to deny that in a general form it has received the widest assent from theology. But if science is satisfied, even in a general way, with its theory of the method of creation, "assent" is a cold word for theology to welcome it with. It is needless at this time of day to point out the surpassing grandeur of the new conception. How it has filled the Christian imagination and kindled to enthusiasm the soberest scientific minds is known to all. For that splendid hypothesis we cannot be too grateful to science, and that theology can only enrich itself which gives it even temporary place. There is a sublimity about the old doctrine of creation—we are speaking of its scientific aspects—which, if one could compare sublimities, is not surpassed by the new; but there is also a baldness. Fulfilments in this direction were sure to come with time, and they have come almost before the riper mind had felt its need of them. The doctrine of evolution fills a gap at the very beginning of our religion, and no one who looks now at the transcendent spectacle of the world's past, as disclosed by science, will deny that it has filled it worthily. Yet, after all, its beauty is not the only part of its contribution to Christianity. Scientific theology required a new view, though it did not require it to come in so magnificent a form. What it wanted was a credible presentation, in view especially of astronomy, geology, and biology. These had made the former theory simply untenable. And science has supplied theology with a theory which the intellect can accept and which for the devout mind leaves everything more worthy of worship than before.

From the contemplation of the flood of light poured by science over the doctrine of Creation, we might pass on to mark the effect upon many other theological truths which rays from the same source are beginning to illuminate. Nothing could be more interesting than to trace up the doctrines one by one in order, and watch the light gradually stealing over all. This must always be a beautiful sight; for this is the light of nature, and even its dawn is lovely. We should like to mark where the last ray gilded the last hill-top, and see how many higher peaks lay still beyond in shadow. And then we should like to prophesy that another light will rise, when physical science is dim, to illuminate what remains. We do not mean an inspired word, but a further contribution from nature itself. To many men of science, judging by the small esteem in which they hold philosophy, the day of mental science apparently is past. To an enlightened theology it is the science of the future. It were strange indeed, and a contradiction of evolution, if the science of atoms and cells were a later or further development than the science of man. Theology sees the point at which physical science must cease to help it; but encouraged by that help, it will expect a science to arise to carry it through the darkness that remains. The analogies of biology may be looked to to elucidate the mysterious phenomena of regeneration. When theology has received its full contribution from natural science it will be able to present to the world a scientific account of its greatest fact. The ultimate mystery of life, whether natural or spiritual, may still remain: but the laws, if not the processes, of the second birth will take their place in that great circle of the known which science is slowly redeeming from the surrounding darkness. We shall then have an embryology, a morphology, and a physiology of the new man; and a scientific theology will add to its departments a higher biology. But this cannot exhaust theology any more than biology exhausts the accounts of the natural man. Further contributions must come in from higher sciences, and different classes of facts must be arrayed under other laws. Theology, therefore, predicates a science of man which is yet to come. There is nothing external to theology; it must collate the different revelations in mind and matter, as science gathers them, one by one. The sciences are but so many natural history collectors, busy over all the world of nature and of thought in gathering material for the final classification by the final science. Without theology, the sciences are incomplete, and theology can only complete itself by completing the sciences.

But we have only space at present to note one or two other examples of the contribution of physical science, and these of a somewhat general kind. One shall be the doctrine of revelation itself. That science shows the necessity for a revelation in a new way, and even hints at subtle analogies for the mode in which it is conveyed to human minds, are points well worth developing. But we can only deal now with the more familiar question of subject-matter and see how that has been affected by evolution.

According to science, as we have already seen, evolution is the method of creation. Now, creation is a form of revelation; it is the oldest form of revelation, the most accessible, the most universal, and still an ever-increasing source of theological truth. It is with this revelation that science begins. If then science, familiar with this revelation, and knowing it to be an evolution, were to be told of the existence of another revelation—an inspired word—it would expect that this other revelation would also be an evolution. Such an anticipation might or might not be justified; but from the law of the uniformity of nature, there would be, to a man of science, a very strong presumption in favour of any revelation which bore this scientific hall-mark, which indicated, that is to say, that God's word had unfolded itself to men like His works.

Now, if science searches the field of theology for an additional revelation, it will find a Bible awaiting it—a Bible in two forms. The one is the Bible as it was presented to our forefathers: the other is the Bible of modern theology. The books, the chapters, the verses, and the words, are the same in each; yet in form they are two entirely different Bibles. To science the difference is immediately palpable. Judging of each of them from its own standpoint, science perceives after a brief examination that the distinction between them is one with which it has been long familiar. In point of fact, the one is constructed like the world according to the old cosmogonies, while the other is an evolution. The one represents revelation as having been produced on the creative hypothesis, the Divine-fiat hypothesis, the ready-made hypothesis; the other on the slow growth or evolution theory. It is at once obvious which of them science would prefer—it could no more accept the first than it could accept the ready-made theory of the universe.

Nothing could be more important than to assure science that the same difficulty has for some time been felt, and with quite equal keenness, by theology. The scientific method in its hand, scientific theology has been laboriously working at a reconstruction of biblical truth from this very view-point of development. And it no more pledges itself to-day to the interpretations of the Bible of a thousand years ago than does science to the interpretations of nature in the time of Pythagoras. Nature is the same to-day as in the time of Pythagoras, and the Bible is the same to-day as a thousand years ago. But the Pythagorean interpretation of nature is not less objectionable to the modern mind than are many ancient interpretations of the Scriptures to the scientific theologian.

The supreme contribution of Evolution to Religion is that it has given it a clearer Bible. One great function of science is, not, as many seem to suppose, to make things difficult, but to make things plain. Science is the great explainer, the great expositor, not only of nature, but of everything it touches. Its function is to arrange things, and make them reasonable. And it has arranged the Bible in a new way, and made it as different as science has made the world. It is not going too far to say that there are many things in the Bible which are hard to reconcile with our ideas of a just and good God. This is only expressing what even the most devout and simple minds constantly feel, and feel to be sorely perplexing, in reading especially the Old Testament. But these difficulties arise simply from an old-fashioned or unscientific view of what the Bible is, and are similar to the difficulties found in nature when interpreted either without the aid of science, or with the science of many centuries ago. We see now that the mind of man has been slowly developing, that the race has been gradually educated, and that revelation has been adapted from the first to the various and successive stages through which that development passed. Instead, therefore, of reading all our theology into Genesis, we see only the alphabet there. In the later books we see primers—first, second, and

third: the truths stated provisionally as for children, but gaining volume
and clearness as the world gets older. Centuries and centuries pass, and
the mind of the disciplined race is at last deemed ripe enough to receive
New Testament truth, and the revelation culminates in the person of
Christ.

The moral difficulties of the Old Testament are admittedly great. But
when approached from the new standpoint, when they are seen to be
rudiments spoken and acted in strange ways to attract and teach children,
they vanish one by one. For instance, we are told that the iniquities of the
father are to be visited upon the children unto the third and fourth
generation. The impression upon the early mind undoubtedly must have
been that this was a solemn threat which God would carry out in anger
in individual cases. We now know, however, that this is simply the
doctrine of heredity. A child inherits its parents' nature not as a special
punishment, but by natural law. In those days that could not be
explained. Natural law was a word unknown; and the truth had to be put
provisionally in a form that all could understand. And even many of the
miracles may have explanations in fact or in principle, which, without
destroying the idea of the miraculous, may show the naturalness of the
supernatural.

The theory of the Bible, which makes belief in revelation possible to the
man of science, Christianity owes to the scientific method. It is not
suggested that the evolution theory in theology was introduced to satisfy
the mind of the scientific thinker, any more than that his appreciation of
it is the test of its truth. As regards the latter, it is to be weighed on its
own evidence and judged by its fruits; and as regards the question of
origin, its ancestry is much more reputable, for it was not a concession to
any theory, but rose out of the facts themselves. Indeed, long before
evolution was formulated in science, discerning minds had seen, with an
enthusiasm which few could at that time share, the slow, steady, upward
growth of theological truth to ever higher and nobler forms. "Wonderful
it is to see with what effort, hesitation, suspense, interruption—with how
many swayings to the right and to the left—with how many reverses, yet
with what certainty of advance, with what precision in its march, and
with what ultimate completeness, it has been evolved; till the whole truth,
'self-balanced on its centre hung,' part answering to part, one, absolute,
integral, indissoluble, while the whole lasts! Wonderful to see how heresy
has but thrown this idea into fresh forms, and drawn out from it further
developments, with an exuberance which exceeded all questionings, and
a harmony which baffled all criticism." These are not the words of modern
science. They were written forty years ago by John Henry Newman. Since
then the central idea of this passage, which though it does not refer to the
Bible is equally applicable to it, has been carried into departments of
theology, in ways which were then undreamed of; and however physical
science may have contributed to this result, it is certain that the method
is not the creation of science.

Evolution is the ever-recurring theme in theology as in nature. We
might indeed almost have grouped the entire contribution of science to

Christianity around this point. The mere presence of the doctrine of Evolution in science has reacted as by an electric induction on every surrounding circle of thought. Whether we like it or not, whether we shun the charge, or court it, or dread it, it has come, and we must set ourselves to understand it. No truth now can remain unaffected by evolution. We can no longer take out a doctrine in this century or in that, bottle it like a vintage, and store it in our creeds. We see truth now as a profound ocean still, but with a slow and ever rising tide. Theology must reckon with this tide. We can store this truth in our vessels, for the formulation of doctrine must never, never stop, but the vessels, with their mouths open, must remain in the ocean. If we take them out the tide cannot rise in them, and we shall only have stagnant doctrines rotting in a dead theology. But theology, surely, with its great age, its eternal foundation, and its countless mysteries, has the least to lose and the most to gain from every advance of knowledge And the development theory has done more for theology perhaps than for any other science. Evolution has given to theology some wholly new departments. It has raised it to a new rank among the sciences. It has given it a vastly more reasonable body of truth, about God and man, about sin and salvation. It has lent it a firmer base, an enlarged horizon, and a richer faith. But its general contribution, on which all these depend, is to the doctrine of revelation.

What then does this mean for revelation? It means in plain language that Evolution has given Christianity a new Bible. Its peculiarity is, that in its form it is like the world in which it is found. It is a word, but its root is now known, and we have other words from the same root. Its substance is still the unchanged language of heaven, yet it is written in a familiar tongue. The new Bible is a book whose parts, though not of unequal value, are seen to be of different kinds of value; where the casual is distinguished from the essential, the local from the universal, the subordinate from the primal end. This Bible is not a book which has been made; it has grown. Hence it is no longer a mere wordbook, nor a compendium of doctrines, but a nursery of growing truths. It is not an even plane of proof text without proportion or emphasis, or light and shade; but a revelation varied as nature, with the Divine in its hidden parts, in its spirit, its tendencies, its obscurities, and its omissions. Like nature it has successive strata, and valley and hilltop, and mist and atmosphere, and rivers which are flowing still, and here and there a place which is desert, and fossils too, whose crude forms are the stepping-stones to higher things. It is a record of inspired deeds as well as of inspired words, an ascending series of inspired facts in a matrix of human history.

Now it is to be marked that this is not the product of any destructive movement, nor is this transformed book in any sense a mutilated Bible. All this has taken place, it may be, without the elimination of a book or the loss of an important word. It is simply the transformation by a method whose main warrant is that the book lends itself to it.

It may be said, and for a time it will continue to be said, that the Christian does not need a transformed Bible; and fortunately, or in some cases unfortunately, this is the case. For years yet the old Bible will continue to nourish the soul of the Church, as it has nourished it in the past; and the needy heart will in all time manage to feed itself apart from any forms. But there is a class, and an ever-increasing class, to whom the form is much. Theology is only beginning to realize how radical is the change in mental attitude of those who have learned to think from science. Intercourse with the ways of nature breeds a mental attitude of its own. It is an attitude worthy of its master. In this presence the student is face to face with what is real. He is looking with his own eyes at facts—at what God did. He finds things in nature just as its Maker left them; and from ceaseless contact with phenomena which will not change for man, and with laws which he has never known to swerve, he fears to trust his mind to anything less. Now this Bible which has been described is the presentation to this age of men who have learned this habit. They have studied the facts, they have looked with their own eyes at what God did; and they are giving us a book which is more than the devout man's Bible, though it is as much as ever the devout man's Bible. It is the apologist's Bible. It is long since the apologist has had a Bible. The Bible of our infancy was not an apologist's Bible. There are things in the Old Testament cast in his teeth by sceptics, to which he has simply no answer. These are the things, the miserable things, the masses have laid hold of. They are the stock-in-trade to-day of the free-thought platform, and the secularist pamphleteer. And, surprising as it is, there are not a few honest seekers who are made timid and suspicious, not a few on the outskirts of Christianity who are kept from coming further in, by the half-truths which a new exegesis, a re-consideration of the historic setting, and a clearer view of the moral purposes of God, would change from barriers into bulwarks of the faith. Such a Bible scientific theology is giving us, and it cannot be proclaimed to the mass of the people too soon. It is no more fair to raise and brandish objections to the Bible without first studying carefully what scientific theologians have to say on the subject, than it would be fair for one who derived his views of the natural world from Pythagoras to condemn all science. It is expected in criticisms of science that the critic's knowledge should at least be up to date, that he is attacking what science really holds; and the same justice is to be awarded to the science of theology. When science makes its next attack upon theology, if indeed that shall ever be again, it will find an armament, largely furnished by itself, which has made the Bible as impregnable as nature.

One question, finally, will determine the ultimate worth of this contribution to Christianity. Does it help it practically? Does it impoverish or enrich the soul? Does it lower or exalt God? These questions with regard to one or two of the elementary truths of religion have been partially answered already. But a closing illustration from the highest of all will show that here also science is not silent.

Science has nothing finer to offer Christianity than the exaltation of its supreme conception—God. Is it too much to say that in a practical age like the present, when the idea and practice of worship tend to be forgotten, God should wish to reveal Himself afresh in ever more striking ways? Is it too much to say, that at this distance from creation, with the eye of theology resting largely upon the incarnation and work of the man Christ Jesus, the Almighty should design with more and more impressiveness to utter Himself as the Wonderful, the Counsellor, the Great and Mighty God? Whether this be so or not, it is certain that every step of science discloses the attributes of the Almighty with a growing magnificence. The author of Natural Religion tells us that "the average scientific man worships just at present a more awful, and as it were a greater Deity than the average Christian." Certain it is that the Christian view and the scientific view together frame a conception of the object of worship, such as the world in its highest inspiration has never reached before. The old student of natural theology rose from his contemplation of design in nature with heightened feeling of the wisdom, goodness, and power, of the Almighty. But never before had the attributes of eternity, and immensity, and infinity, clothed themselves with language so majestic in its sublimity. It is a language for the mind alone. Yet in the presence of the slow toiling of geology, millennium after millennium, at the unfinished earth; before the unthinkable past of palaeontology, both but moments and lightning-flashes to the immenser standards of astronomy: before these even the imagination reels and leaves an experience only for religion.

Spiritual Diagnosis

An Argument for Placing the Study of the Soul on a Scientific Basis

Essay read before the Theological Society, New College, Edinburgh, November, 1873.

The study of the soul in health and disease ought to be as much an object of scientific study and training as the health and diseases of the body.

It has long been one of the favourite axioms of Apologetics, that a Christian life is the best argument for Christianity. And, if an old argument, it is after all the best argument, for in these last days there is nothing in the philosophy of apologetical religion at all worth reviving compared with this living power of true lives. A freethinker may go very far without meeting an argument to throw him back upon his own inner soul, but no one can live long, be he in high life or low life, without coming within the influence of a Christian man. The power of the individual, the value of the unit, the respect due to one human soul—this is the great truth for churches, for armies, and for empires. Students of the new science of sociology may deny this truth as they will, and their great disciple, Herbert Spencer, may denounce what he calls the "great-man-theory of history" as only fit for savages gossiping round their camp fire, but it still remains a great and important truth (as he himself expresses it before failing to refute it) "that throughout the past of the human race the doings of conspicuous persons have been the only things worthy of remembrance."

The past has indeed no masses. Men, not masses, have done all that is great in history, in science, and in religion. The New Testament itself is but a brief biography; and many pages of the Old are marked by the lives of men. Yet it is just this truth which we require to be taught again to-day—to be content with aiming at units. Every atom in the universe can act on every other atom, but only through the atom next it. And if a man would act upon every other man, he can do so best by acting, one at a time, upon those beside him. The true worker's world is a unit.

Recognise the personal glory and dignity of the unit as an agent. Work with units, but, above all, work at units.

But the capacity of acting upon individuals is now almost a lost art. It is hard to learn again. We have spoilt ourselves by thinking to draw thousands by public work—by what people call "pulpit eloquence," by platform speeches, and by convocations and councils, Christian conferences, and by books of many editions. We have been painting Madonnas and Ecce Homos and choirs of angels, like Raphael, and it is hard to condescend to the beggar boy of Murillo. Yet we must begin again, and begin far down. Christianity began with one. We have forgotten the simple way of the Founder of the greatest influence the world has ever seen—how He ran away from cities, how He shirked mobs, how He lagged behind the rest at Samaria to have a quiet talk with one woman at a well, how He stole away from crowds and entered into the house of one humble Syro-Phoenician woman, "and would have no man know it." In small groups of twos and threes He collected the early Church around Him. One by one the disciples were called—and there were only twelve in all. We all know well enough how to move the masses; we know how to draw a crowd round us, but to attract the units—that is the hard matter. Teach us how to fascinate the unit by our glance, by our conversational oratory, by our mystery of sympathy! We know how to bring the mob about us, how to flash and storm in passion, how to work in the appeal at the right moment, how to play upon all the figures of rhetoric in succession, and how to throw in a calm when no one expects, but every one wants it. Every one knows this, or can know it easily; but to draw souls one by one, to buttonhole them and steal from them the secret of their lives, to talk them clean out of themselves, to read them off like a page of print, to pervade them with your spiritual essence and make them transparent, this is the spiritual science which is so difficult to acquire and so hard to practise.

"After a spirit of discernment," says an old French Sage (La Bruyere), "the next rarest thing in the world are diamonds and pearls." Of the three elements, body, mind, and soul, which make up a responsible human being, two only have been hitherto treated as fit subjects for scientific inquiry. From six thousand years of contemplation of the phenomena of human life and thought, only two sciences have emerged. Physiology has told us all that is possible of the human body; psychology, of the mind. But the half is not accounted for. We wish, further, a spiritual psychology to tell us of the unseen realities of the soul. This is where our University training must be supplemented. It deals with man as a body and a mind. It forgets that man is a trinity. It is an extraordinary and momentous fact that by far the most important factor in human life has been up to this time all but altogether ignored by the thinking world. Of course every religious writer has a few notions upon the subject, but notions are not enough. If the mind is large enough and varied enough to make a philosophy of mind possible, is the soul such a trifling part of man that it is not worth while seeking to frame a science of it?—a science of it which men can learn, and which can be a guide and help in practice to all who feel an interest in the deepest thing in human life? It is no use to say there is no special soul—that there is a strange never-comprehended essence, half emotion, half affection, half reason, half unearthliness, to attempt to analyse which would only leave us, like Milton's philosophic angels, "in wandering mazes lost." But this is the mere concealment of ignorance in mystery. There is a soul, and there is a spiritual life. Plato knew it and called it, in his wonderment over it, "the soulish mind." Solomon knew it when he talked of "the hearing ear." Addison knew it and defined it: "'Tis the divinity that stirs within us." And in "Culture and Religion" the Principal of St. Andrew's University charges his students "that there is a faculty of spiritual apprehension which is very different from those which are trained in schools and colleges, which must be educated and fed not less but more carefully than our lower faculties, else it will be starved and die."

The same thoughtful writer has put the problem which we are endeavouring to meet in plain and forcible terms. "But because the primary truths of religion," he says, "refuse to be caught in the grip of the logical vice—because they are transcendent, and only mystically apprehended, are thinking men therefore either to give up these subjects as impossible to think about or to content themselves with a vague religiosity, an unreal sentimentalism?" The Principal's question is a striking question. Are we content to let this great spiritual life work silently around us without attempting to know more about it, to analyze it, to make it more accessible to us and us to it? Are we to regard it as some weird element, unapproachable, mysterious, unstable, incomprehensible in its essence? There is, it is true, an element about it which keeps us at our distance from it; but as its groundwork is human, may we not see the points where it touches the human, the changes it effects, the hindrances to the changes, and the wonderful complexity of action and interaction which it originates? Are there materials here for a philosophy, and is it lawful to reduce it to a science? Can there, in short, be a science of spirituality?

At first sight the idea is repulsive in the extreme. Yet a science is a classification of facts; and is there anything irreverent or presumptuous in attempting to classify the facts of the spiritual life? The facts, it may be answered, are too numerous; they are more than the sand of the sea. But so are the combinations of elements with which the chemist deals, and the modifications of morphological type with which the biologist deals, yet we have a chemistry and a biology. That, then, is the least of the difficulty. But a great one, apparently an insurmountable one, lies just on the threshold. The facts of physical science lie in the order of the natural, and they are finite. The facts of spiritual science, if we may call it so, lie in the order of the supernatural, and they are infinite. They are pervaded by an element which no man can fathom. "The Spirit bloweth where it listeth." We look in a man's soul for that which we saw there yesterday, but the unseen influence has swept across the heart, and the spiritual scenery is changed. The man himself is the same, his passions unaltered in their strength, his foibles unchanged in their weakness, but the furniture of the soul has been moved, and the spiritual machinery goes on upon a new and suddenly developed principle. Here, then, our investigations are stopped at the outset. Dare we approach no nearer? Often we would fain do so. Often we are placed in such circumstances that plainly we must do so. A friend is in trouble, we are in trouble. But how are we to proceed? What guide have we in ministering to a soul diseased?

Is there no guide-book upon the subject, no chart or table of the logical history of the spiritual life, no chair of Spiritual Diagnosis? We do not mean a table such as Doddridge has given us in "The Rise and Progress of Religion in the Soul." The fatal error of that style of work is to give the inquiring soul the idea of a certain mechanical process to be passed through before conversion can be attained. But conversion does not always develop like a proposition in Euclid, or sensitized plate in photography. God the Creator will have no machine-made men in earth or heaven. And it is not His will that there should only be a few stereotyped forms of saints—the Richard Baxter type, the Jeremy Taylor type, and the Philip Doddridge type. Therefore it is a dangerous thing to put forms and processes, which exist only in the logical imagination, into the hands of the inquirer. But when these works are put into the hands of the Christian teacher or minister, their utility is beyond all praise. He, as spiritual adviser, should be thoroughly acquainted with the rationale of conversion. He should know it as a physician his pharmacopoeia. He should know every phase of the human soul, in health and disease, in the fulness of joy and the blackness of despair. He should know the "Pilgrim's Progress" better than Bunyan. The scheme of salvation, as we are accustomed to call it, should be ever clearly defined in his consciousness. The lower stages, the period of transition, its solemnity, its despairs, its glimmering light, its growing faith; and the Christian life begun, the laborious working out in fear and trembling, the slavish scrupulosity, still the fearfulness of fall, still remorse, more faith, more hope; and last of all the higher spiritual life, the realization of freedom, the disappearance of the slavish scrupulosity, the pervasion of the whole life with God.

Such a skeleton is easily made and easily remembered, and it is all that many have to perform their work with; but it is no more adequate for its great task than is the compass of a schoolboy's whistle to take in the sweep of Handel's "Messiah." To fill up such an outline with all the exquisite tracery of thought and emotion and doubt, which develop within the mind of an inquiring soul, is a great and rare talent; and to apply such knowledge in the practice of daily life is a power which scarce one will be found to possess. Let not any think that such knowledge is easily attained; nor have many attained it. The men to whom you or I would go if spiritual darkness spread across our souls, who are they? How few have penetration enough to diagnose our case, to observe our least apparent symptoms, to get out of us what we had resolved not to tell them, to see through and through us the evil and the good. Plenty there are to preach to us, but who will interview us, and anatomize us, and lay us bare to God's eye and our own? X won't be preached to along with Y and Z and Q; that won't do X any good, for he thinks it is all meant for Y, Z, and Q. But to take X by himself; to feel his pulse alone, and give him one particular earnest word—the only one word that would do—all to himself—this is the simple feat which we look in vain for men to perform. There is a tendency piously to leave such matters to God, and say they are quite safe in His hands, who alone searcheth the heart. But He hath appointed us to be our brother's keeper, nor will He do for my brother what could be done by me. We cannot expect the Spirit's help to teach us what only laziness and personal indifference hinder us from learning; and to despise a power which He gave us capacities to possess is not the way to show that we trust Him who gave it. "Placeat homini quidquid Deo placet."

This study of the soul, in which I am endeavouring to enlist your interest, is a difficult study. It is difficult, because the soul as far transcends the mind in complexity and in variety as the mind the body. The soul is an infinitely large subject—an infinitely deep and mysterious subject. The chemist in his intricate analysis deals not with elements more subtle and evasive

"Ay, men may wonder while they scan
A living, thinking, feeling man."

But we do not need to go to Mrs. Browning, or to "Hamlet," to be told "What a piece of work is man!" Apart altogether from the religious element in him, he is still the greatest mystery of science. Every man is a problem to every other man—much more every spiritual man. It is hard to know a man's brain, and harder to know his feelings; but hardest of all to know his religious convictions. It is hard to know the deepest that a man has. A well-known American essayist and poet has told us that the difficulty of analyzing our neighbour's character arises from the fact that every man is in reality a threefold man. When two persons are in conversation, there are really six persons in conversation. Thus, to put the paradox into the shape of an example, suppose that John and Tom are in conversation, there are three Johns and three Toms, who are accounted for in this way:

Three Johns

1. The real John; known only to his Maker.

2. John's ideal John; John, i.e., as he thinks himself; never the real John, and often very unlike him.

3. Tom's ideal John; i.e., John as Tom thinks him; never the real John, nor John's John, but often very unlike either.

Three Toms

1. The real Tom.

2. Tom's ideal Tom.

3. John's ideal Tom.

In this way when I talk to another it is not me that he hears talking, but his ideal of me; nor do I talk to him as he defines himself, but to my ideal of him. Now that ideal will, without almost inconceivable care and penetration on my part, be quite different also from his real self as God only knows him, so that instead of speaking to his real soul, I may possibly be speaking to his ideal of his own soul, or more likely to my ideal of it.

From this it will be seen at a glance that the power of soul analysis is a hard thing to possess oneself of. It requires intense discrimination and knowledge of human nature—much and deep study of human life and character. The man with whom you speak being made up of two ideals—his own and yours, and one real—God's, it is one of the hardest possible tasks to abandon your ideal of him and get to know the real—God's. Then having known it so far as possible to man, there remains the greatest difficulty of all—to introduce him to himself. You have created a new man for him, and he will not recognise him at first. He can see no resemblance to his ideal self; the new creature is not such a lovely picture as he would like to own; the lines are harshly drawn, and there is little grace and no poetry in it. But he must be told that none of us are what we seem; and if he would deal faithfully with himself, he must try to see himself differently from what he seems. Then he must be led with much delicacy to make a little introspection of himself; and with the mirror lifted to his own soul you read off together some of the indications which are defining themselves vaguely upon its surface. Even in social and domestic circles the difficulty of performing this apparently simple operation upon human nature is so keenly felt that scarce one friend will be found with a friendship true enough to perform it to another. And in religious matters it will be at once conceded that the complexity of the difficulties increases the problem a hundredfold.

There is a danger, however—speaking next of the more directly religious aspects of the question—in exaggerating these difficulties; and, indeed, the further objection may have occurred to some minds that, by attaching so much importance to the human power we take away the one great element in salvation—its Divine freeness through the grace of God.

Is not religion for the poor and illiterate? is not the way easy to find? Thank God it is so! So little can man do to enlighten it. But he can do something, and he ought to do more. In this more than in anything else he is his brother's keeper. Not for himself does man live. Every action of every man has an ancestry and a posterity—an ancestry and a posterity in other lives. "Each reads his fate in the other's eyes," says Emerson. "I am a part of all that I have met," says Tennyson. And how do you explain that most wonderful phenomenon which is as surprising a contemplation to some minds as the thought of eternity itself—the silence of God? God keeping silence! And man doubting and sinning and repenting all alone, and groping blindfold after truth, and losing his way and working out his salvation with painful trembling and fear! It is an unfathomable mystery; but may it not be, in small part, just for this that, on the one hand, God offers man the glory and honour of sharing His work; and on the other, that He wishes human souls to be graven with the marks of other human souls in all their free and infinite variety? God is a God of variety. No two leaves are the same, no two sand grains, no two souls. And as the universe would be but a poor affair if every leaf were the counterpart of the oak leaf or the birch, so would the spiritual world present but a sorry spectacle if we were all duplicates of John Calvin. Therefore has God made room for individual action in the building up of His kingdom upon earth; and therefore it is not a presumption but a duty for every man to be moulding and making the souls around him, to be perfecting and guiding his own faculties for this great work.

The great danger in doing this work, next to doing it without any education for it, is to overdo it. In dealing with a case which is once put into our hands we are apt to consider it too much of a professional and personal matter. Our influence has become too conscious. We have found what a powerful thing it may become, and we seek a "reputation for influence." Thus our pride is smitten if success does not at once crown our efforts, and we attempt to second them by unlawful means. We assume the didactic when we should simply be attractive or suggestive. We encourage the favourable and forget to notice an unfavourable symptom. We supply allopathic when prudence would suggest homoeopathic doses. And finally, we assume too much upon ourselves, forgetting that we are but fellow-workers together with God, and by taking too officious an interest, the individual, making nothing of it, is apt to throw the responsibility of non-success upon us, and so spoil not only our whole influence with others, but his own chance of being bettered in the future by others.

There are also limits to the exercise of this power which are as yet not well defined, and which rest at present upon no religio-philosophic basis, but on mere empiricism. The whole subject, indeed, rests in the meantime only upon the merest individual empiricism; and it is a matter of profound regret that so sacred and important a subject should exist in such a dishevelled state when the scientific method, which is being applied to so many trivial matters, could be so easily applied to it. We can conceive of some minds being deeply shocked to hear of scientific observations being taken on a human soul, and adjustments made to it, and results calculated as if it were a mere question of spectrum analysis. But the irreverence is only in the words. We do wish a scientific treatment of the subject; and if there is anything to sadden and humble in the contemplation of the religious work of the day, it is the thought of the crude and slipshod treatment of one of the most sacred subjects in the religious life.

We are not ignoring the power of God in conversion by not speaking of it. You say He can work with the roughest tools even on the finest of marbles. Without denying it, He would not polish diamonds on grindstones if He could get lapidaries to do it better. It won't do to talk religiously, or complacently, or blasphemously of trusting in Him when we are too lazy to qualify ourselves for being worth the using in His service. Don't fear that we shall become too acute at diagnosing and prescribing for souls, and so take the matter out of God's hands.

And now, in conclusion, as to the great subject of the training and exercise of the power of spiritual discernment, what is it possible for us to say? We can indeed but guess at it. Those who have thought of it have confessed that everything yet remains to be done. Thus one of the keenest minds of New England has said, "The school of the future may be called a Life School, whose object is to study the strength and weakness of human nature minutely, . . . to understand men, and to deal with them face to face, and heart to heart, . . . and in regard to such a school as this, while there has been much done incidentally, the revised procedure of education yet awaits development and accomplishment." Henry Ward Beecher, in his Yale lecture (on preaching), has given to this subject perhaps by far the most valuable popular contribution of the age. His chapter on the study of Human Nature is especially discriminating, and only the knowledge that there must now be few into whose hands that work has not fallen prevents us stealing time to make lengthened quotations. (Let two suffice, page 85 and page 94.) Beecher, had he been less of a preacher and more of a pastor, could have been one of the greatest students of the soul. As it is, he is surpassed by few, perhaps by none in this country, only by Dr. Spencer in his own. Spurgeon is not so much of a practical analyst as a self-introspectionist. So also were Thomas a Kempis and Blaise Pascal, and pious John Hervey and quaint Robert Bruce, and so also in a sense were Dr. Duncan and Dr. Goulburn, who has done for spirituality what Burton did for melancholy. The Puritan writers, and pre-eminent among them Baxter and Owen, were skilled analysts of human nature, but they seem to have applied their power more in the pulpit than the pew. In this respect, too, Bunyan was quite unsurpassed, and in some of his sermons, specially his famous "last" one, the most masterly specimens of this kind of work are to be found.

Yet with all this perfection there was always something wrong about these men from the practical point of view. They knew so much about humanity that they had lost what of it they had themselves in the pursuit of it in others. Although they are always called practical hands, they are only so in a gross sense. They were most of them wanting in that delicacy of handling which makes analysis effective instead of insulting; and many of the Puritans were quite destitute of the foremost quality which distinguishes the successful diagnosist—respect, veneration even, for the soul of another. A man may be ever so gross and vulgar, but when you come to deal with the deepest that is in him, he becomes sensitive and feminine. Brusqueness and an impolite familiarity may do very well when dealing with his brains, but without tenderness and courtesy you can only approach his heart to shock it. The whole of etiquette is founded on respect; and by far the highest and tenderest etiquette is the etiquette of soul and soul.

To know and remember the surpassing dignity of the human soul—for its own sake, for its great Godlike elements, for its immortality, above all for His sake who made it and gave Himself for it—this is the first axiom to be remembered. Many men study men, but not to sympathize with them: the lawyer for gain, the artist for fame, the actor for applause, the novelist for profession. How well up is the actor in plot and passion and intrigue! how deftly can the novelist anatomize love and jealousy, vengeance and hate! And when there are men found to study human nature for its own sake, or for filthy lucre's sake, shall there be none to do it for man's sake—for God's sake? There is one great reason why the ministry of so many great and holy men has been so far from being what is called a converting ministry. We read their biographies, and shrink into nothingness at the contemplation of such holiness and saintliness of life as we had never dreamed possible to man, and we marvel, and greatly, that one irreligious, unconverted man should be left in the whole countryside; but we find indeed that their parish was no better than its neighbours. And the explanation is plain. Those men laboured under a terrible disease—it is called Theophobia—the name explains itself. A minister catches it, and his power is gone. Men are awed by it, venerate it as they venerate few things else. They will speak of it and praise it, but never imitate it. It is a grand but useless spectacle. Those who have it become wrapped up in one subject; and though that be the highest of all, it is nevertheless a monstrosity when followed to the exclusion of everything else. The sympathies of these men are all and always Godwards. They are always vindicating God. Their whole atmosphere is of God. They have left earth before their time. They have left human nature in the lurch; they have forgotten humanity, and humanity can no longer profit by them, it can only wonder at them. Their thoughts go always straight up to God, and are never healthy enough to be refracted upon man. Now to get to God is a high thing, but they only get at one side of Him. They don't see over to the other side, which is inclined towards man. Yet to get to man by way of God, and God by way of man, is the only way to keep the entire health of the soul.

We have much yet to say of this study, but the subject must end almost before it is begun. The one great thing is to study life earnestly and practically and realistically.

* * * * *

We must aim at the manly and sturdy type of the religious diagnosist; we must try to be, as Oliver Wendell Holmes forcibly says, "a man that knows men in the street, at their work, human nature in its shirt sleeves—who makes bargains with deacons instead of talking over texts with them, and a man who has found out that there are plenty of praying rogues and swearing saints in the world."

One thing I can assure you of. If any man develops this faculty of reading others, of reading them in order to profit by them, he will never be without practice. Men do not say much about these things, but the amount of spiritual longing in the world at the present moment is absolutely incredible. No one can ever even faintly appreciate the intense spiritual unrest which seethes everywhere around him; but one who has tried to discern, who has begun by private experiment, by looking into himself, by taking observations upon the people near him and known to him, has witnessed a spectacle sufficient to call for the loudest and most emphatic action. Gentlemen, I have but vaguely hinted at this subject; I venture to think it a question of vital interest, giving life a mission, giving a new and burning interest even to the most commonplace surroundings, and opening up a field for lifelong study and effort.

www.ingramcontent.com/pod-product-compliance
Lightning Source LLC
Chambersburg PA
CBHW051847040426

42447CB00006B/738